*To be perfectly united to
a woman is man's greatest
fulfillment and his finest success,
bar none.*

IN
SEARCH
OF A
HELP MEET

FOR THOSE SEEKING THEIR FOREVER LOVE-MATE

www.nogreaterjoy.org

We'd love to hear what God has done in your life through the reading of this book. Contact us at www.nogreaterjoy.org or write us at the address listed below.

In Search of a Help Meet
Copyright © 2013 by Michael & Debi Pearl

ISBN: 978-1-61644-050-3

First printing: January 2013 - 10,000

Visit www.NoGreaterJoy.org for information on this and other products produced by No Greater Joy Ministries.

Requests for information should be addressed to:
No Greater Joy Ministries Inc., 1000 Pearl Road, Pleasantville, TN 37033 USA.

All scripture quotations are taken from the King James Holy Bible.

Cover design: Shoshanna Easling, Aaron Aprile
Layout: Karen Sargent
Cover photo: iStockphoto.com

Printed in the United States of America

Psalm 30:12

"To the end that
my glory may sing praise
to thee, and not be silent.
O LORD my God,
I will give thanks unto thee
for ever."

CONTENTS

Love and marriage
are the best things
this side of heaven.

THE REASON WHY

As I write this book, I have been married to the wife of my youth for over forty-one years, and I can tell you that love and marriage are the best things this side of heaven. They are the context by which all other things are experienced and appreciated. If I were not married to my little lady, I wouldn't be half the man I am today; I would be something less than one quarter.

When I was a young man, seventeen to twenty-five years old, I had many friends running the race of life alongside me, many of whom appeared to have greater prospects than I. But as I look back forty years I see that our lives were defined by the women we married. The road forked when we took wives, and from that point forward some of us went on to a glorious life while others started a downhill slide that came to be characterized by sadness and even tragedy. A woman can make all the difference in the rest of your life. Getting the right girl is as important as choosing the right boat when you intend to sail around the world. Over half the marriages taking place in your generation will sink. Others will be torn by the storms of life. Storms can be weathered when two row together, but no one wants to be confined to the boat with a sailing partner who resists your every move, leaving you miserable the entire journey.

Few sail into paradise and remain.

Few sail into paradise and remain. Fewer still reach the finish line having made a difference in the world. Bad marriages can be made much better—some even glorious—but those that start out glorious and remain so year after year are the overcomers whose relationship will become an eternal example of Christ and his church. That is why you need to prayerfully and wisely search for a help meet.

You need to prayerfully and wisely search for a help meet.

The man who lives as if life is a series of maybes, hopes, and whatevers is playing Russian roulette. He is destined for failure. Life is a series of investments and returns. We invest thoughts and actions, and the returns follow.

We eat according to our tastes and preferences; we say what is in our hearts; and we marry the woman to whom we are drawn. The question then arises, what sort of woman will get your attention, your heart, and your lifelong commitment? Just last week a concerned father who has three grown sons of marriageable age mused, "How do you get your sons to look at the right girls? Like a largemouth bass they just chase anything that is shiny and wiggles." My answer: "They will marry what is in their hearts." So choosing the right help meet begins with a wise heart.

If any of you lack wisdom, let him ask of God, that giveth to all men liberally, and upbraideth not; and it shall be given him. James 1:5

Your first step to obtaining a godly wife is prayer. Start this chapter by asking God for his wisdom and understanding.

The question then arises, what sort of woman will you be drawn toward?

*Your life will be
defined by the woman
you marry.*

God created man
with a deep, abiding
need for someone.

Chapter 1

THE HELPER OF YOUR SOUL

Love and marriage are God's idea. Therefore you can count on God to guide, direct, and instruct you as you seek a wife, that is, if you are on good terms with him. You honor God—he blesses you. If you slip around defiling yourself, you can expect nothing from God but judgment. You cannot defile yourself with pornography, video games, and recreational dating and expect God to redeem you by giving you one of his choice virgins. It is God's desire that a man who honors him should find a soul mate his equal. This is God's blessing and design.

Since you are reading this book, you already acknowledge your need for a wife. But do you know how really extensive is your need? It extends far beyond a legitimate sex partner. God created you with a deep, abiding need to merge your soul with one of the fairer sex. Every man needs a best friend, a partner, a faithful buddy, and someone to help him stay focused on all things pure and lovely.

Man's most pressing need is sex.

Although most guys are slow to acknowledge it, they also need someone to help them make wise, balanced decisions. All men need a holy helper.

We are most aware of our need for sex. In my younger years as a single male, whenever I thought of marriage it was always in the context of sex. I tried to think spiritually, but, truthfully, marriage meant one thing: I could have sex any time I wanted and as often as I wanted. After being married a couple weeks I was shocked as I discovered that my own body had limitations. A starving man thinks

God made man to need sex.

he could eat forever. A man well fed doesn't think about food anymore and he has to find something else to think about—and do. Imagination and reality are sometimes far apart. I assume most single young men think the way I did, so I will set your mind at ease and start with the sexual needs of man first.

God made us fellows to need sex; not just want it, but downright gotta have it. It was God who designed sex, not the devil. Sex is not exclusively for having babies; it is our Creator's great gift to us— the biggest bang this side of the pearly gates. It is the reward God wrapped up in marriage: **"and they shall be one flesh."** Gen. 2:24 It is the defining difference between good friends and a married couple. Some guys think their sex drive is the devil in their pants. Not so. The

Sex is designed in such a way that causes a man to intensely search for his mate.

male over thirteen or fourteen years old who doesn't regularly yearn for sex needs a doctor and a serious hormone treatment. It is not the drive, but how you use it that constitutes sin.

The normal sexual drive causes a young man to intensely search for his mate. When a man is young, strong, and busy making his mark, he can sublimate his need for a lifelong best friend. A buddy is fine, but the casual need for companionship never rises to the level of a consuming necessity. It is also nice to have a helper, but you can always hire someone to help you perform chores and conduct business. No young man enjoys having another person around all the time, especially someone who has an opinion about everything and a will that is sometimes contrary, so why would we join ourselves to another person for the rest of our lives? It is obvious. The overwhelming need for sex and intimacy is what compels us to surrender to the shackles of holy matrimony.

God Said

God said, **"It is not good that the man should be alone."** ^{Gen. 2:18} All us guys eventually come to feel a deep, empty, sometimes hungry need, a loneliness, a longing to have someone special with whom we share our most intimate self. It seems like the wait is too long. There is a reason for that. We are following the pattern God set in the garden with the first man. Rather than have the first couple wake up in a three-bedroom, bamboo house in paradise, God created Adam without a woman, all alone in a delightful garden of animals and plants. I share your sentiment; what could possibly be delightful when you are alone with nothing to snuggle up to at night but a cabbage?

Adam's Soul Mate

The first man, lying in his dusty womb, received his first breath from God and opened his eyes to look up into the creation that would be his home. As he rose to view the wonder of his surroundings, he had a conversation with his maker. God told him to dress and keep the garden, and, in the process, he could eat the fruit and nuts from every tree except the one found in the middle of the garden. What young man hasn't dreamed of living in a paradise with a naked woman? But wait…for Adam there was no naked woman or even the knowledge of one. Rather, Adam, all by himself, was given the task of naming all the animals as they passed in review. What a glorious parade that must have been! Except…there was still no Eve.

Apparently, by observing the animals functioning in family and social units, Adam became aware of something missing in his life, so he searched for his counterpart, his helper, someone suitable to meet his needs. **"…but for Adam there was not found an help meet for him."** Genesis 2:20 There it is. Adam, standing in that beautiful garden, surrounded by every kind of animal, knew that he was meant to be part of a unit of two. He felt his God-given need for another person to be the helper of his soul. Paradise is not complete without a pretty

Husband and wife together becoming a complete picture of the Creator is the essence of a glorious marriage.

little partner. That is why we guys get so antsy in our middle to late teens, can't keep our eyes off the girls, and go to church and stare at the back of their heads rather than listen to the preacher. We watch them parade around in their new dresses and are aware every time they fix their hair a little bit different. We can smell them and want to taste them.

They are better than ice cream to a six-year-old. The need is so great, so consuming, so controlling of our every thought that it feels like a sinful addiction. "What is wrong with me? Am I going to hell?" No, but you are catching on fire, and you can't put it out.

Love and marriage between one man and one woman can, with God's blessings, create a paradise. No wonder God said, **"It is not good that the man should be alone."** But all things God created have context. Sex is intended to be the bond and blessing of marriage. All human appetites and passions must be managed and regulated if they are to fulfill the purpose for which they were designed. Sex was designed for marriage and marriage was designed for sex and much, much more.

The sex drive is the greatest temptation known to a 20-year-old man. The apostle Paul spoke of the only cure, saying, **"…it is better to marry than to burn."** 1 Corinthians 7:9 God made you that way. If you didn't "burn" a little, you wouldn't learn your need. So it is not only normal, it's necessary. Adam had to endure it for only a few hours; we have to walk around on fire for ten years or so. It's tough but worth the wait. **"Hope deferred maketh the heart sick: but when the desire cometh, it is a tree of life."** Proverbs 13:12 Good things come to those who wait. Your first responsibility in obtaining a beautiful help meet is to wait upon the LORD and honor him so that he can guide and bless you with his best.

Completed

I started thinking of having a girl of my very own by the time I was six. I was just a month short of twenty-six years old before I finally got her. It seemed like a tiresome long time between the first stirrings of longing to the passion of puberty and finally to the blessed relief of marriage. God created Adam but delayed providing him with a wife because he wanted the first man to feel his need—not just a sexual need, but the need for a friend, someone to notice and appreciate his handiwork, as well as someone to remind him to keep up the good work. The need for a lifetime partner is part of what makes us human. As men we are not complete, not a final model of the image of God, thus there is in all of us a natural drive to find our completeness. The understanding of this lack grows as we mature. As a man seeks to love and cherish his wife, he will become more and more balanced in his reflection of who God intended him to be. Husband and wife together, becoming a complete picture of the Creator, is the essence of a glorious marriage.

The need for a lifetime partner is part of what makes us human.

TIME TO CONSIDER:

The Bible is not as prudish as the people who read it.

There be three things which are too wonderful for me, yea, four which I know not: The way of an eagle in the air; the way of a serpent upon a rock; the way of a ship in the midst of the sea; and the way of a man with a maid. Proverbs 30:18-19

The first three are natural wonders that stir the mind to consider the beauty and mystery of nature. They are mentioned only as metaphors to illustrate the last, "the way of a man with a maid." The three examples from nature are indeed wonders, but the fourth goes so far beyond wonder that it leaves the writer declaring it unfathomable.

Who has not stood and watched the eagle effortlessly soar in the heavens with grace and dignity and not envied his gift of flight, wondering what our cumbersome world looks like from his lofty perspective?

Back down to earth, the serpent on the rock is sleek, shiny, and sensual, lazily basking in the warm sun, its subtle movements slow and hypnotic, possessing grace and beauty.

In contrast, the ship in the sea is powerful and boisterous as it groans under its full sails, splashing and crashing, driven by unseen forces to a destination far beyond the reach of landlocked lads and lassies.

Similar to these three, a man with a maid soars to great heights and then sensually lies half asleep in the sun, or is possessed of powerful, unseen forces that seem to capture the drama of all nature and sweep him and his maid to mysteries beyond the horizon—and all this by divine design.

**Whoso findeth a wife findeth a good thing, and obtaineth
favour of the LORD.** Proverbs 18:22

Wow! Getting married is a "good thing." Think about it; God
favors the man who takes a wife. Or to put it another way, by getting
married you obtain preferential treatment from God.

You obviously agree with God about needing a woman of your
very own, or you wouldn't still be reading this book. Now, read on to
learn how to find the right one.

God favors the man
who takes a wife.

Chapter 2

WHOM SHOULD I MARRY?

**My son, hear the instruction of thy father, and forsake not
the law of thy mother: For they shall be an ornament of
grace unto thy head, and chains about thy neck.** Proverbs 1:8-9

I Found the Best for Me

How can a sixty-seven-year-old know anything about finding a
help meet? I was sixteen once and in love . . . and seventeen and in
love . . . and seventeen and in love again (different girl each
time) . . . and eighteen and nineteen and so on to twenty-five before I
found my suitable helper.

I was still a virgin when I married my wife, but it wasn't easy
maintaining that virtuous gift. I was always horny. Back then it was
a constant burden; with age it becomes an occasional blessing. I look
back and know it was the grace of God that got me through the
female gauntlet with my virtue intact.

I also know that if I had chosen to marry any one of the other
wonderful girls I knew, my life would not be the same today. I would
be somebody different. My children would be different. My life's
accomplishments would be different. I cannot imagine a better
life—a better marriage—than the one I have lived. I must thank God
that he had his hand in my choice and that he gave me the patience
to wait on his choice.

I even proposed to the wrong girl once. You will read about that in a coming chapter. She said "Yes, but . . . " and then I said "No," and we moved on. Oh, she was a wonderful person by any and all standards, but we would not have made a wonderful marriage. It turns out that as we matured our lives went in different directions. We both became different people. At nineteen and twenty years of age, I could not have anticipated the changes that would occur in each of us. But God knew.

I spent my youth and early twenties searching for the one God had in reserve just for me. I found her when the time was right. While I was waiting on her, God was waiting on me to become the man she needed. I knew her before I loved her, and I loved her before I knew she was the one.

How can you know she is the right one when it is so easy to love so many? That is what this book is all about.

Let Me Pick Your Wife

Are you confused and uncertain? Let me pick your wife for you. I am old and wise and the author of this book on finding a suitable wife. Or maybe you can trust your father's choice, or your mother's. She has a strong opinion and is not afraid to express it. Then again, you could let the church choose for you. They will find a nice daughter of the church and pair you up with their blessings. You are just a dumb kid, so trust the old, wise people in your life—that is, if you want to play Russian roulette with your future.

One of my sons got married before I knew he was looking, so I didn't get a chance to "help" him choose. He did fine without me. But my oldest son, Gabriel, just hung around until I thought he might end up being an old, maidless man. So I got active searching for his help meet. When I was out and about at some Christian event, I always had my eye out for the girl of his dreams. Several times I spotted one who I thought would be just perfect. Typically, I would walk up to the family and say, "I have a son who needs a good wife and wonder if I could have him come visit your family?" I never had one turn me down. "Right to the point" is my motto.

She was always beautiful, smiled so much the sun had to crank up the juice just to match her radiance, intelligent, cheerful, creative, perfect—a lot like my wife. I would come home and tell him about one I had discovered. After contacting the father, he would travel across several states to spend the weekend with the family. When he returned I would ask, "Well, what do you think?"

One time he said, "She was nice; I really liked her father and brothers."

"Well, what about her?" I asked.

"She is a fine girl, but it just didn't click. I wouldn't want to be married to her."

"Why not? What is wrong with her?"

"Nothing. She just doesn't excite me; we could be friends, nothing more."

I liked the girls; why didn't he? Because I selected young girls that would have suited me when I was young and single. He is not me and his tastes are different.

Then, through the instigation of a friend, he discovered a beautiful young lady in a distant state who excited him to the core. I met her and knew she was indeed a fine person, but she was not the girl I would have found interesting when I was twenty-eight. I tried to talk him out of it, but to no avail. He married her and continues to find her delightful. Today she is a wonderful daughter-in-law and an absolutely great mother of three of my most happy and well-behaved grandkids. And she excites him still.

If someone else chooses your bride, he is choosing for himself.

Looking back, I learned a very important lesson that I can now pass on to you. No one, and I mean no one, can choose your wife for you. If someone else chooses, he is choosing for himself.

Several of the girls he passed up became friends of his sisters and of the family, even visiting from time to time. They have married and we have come to know their husbands and children. It is interesting that I would not have chosen their husbands for them either, but today it is obvious that they are perfectly suited to their spouses.

With my vast experience, I can now pass judgment on my wisdom as a matchmaker: it stinks. I am unfit to order another person's entire life by choosing his or her spouse. It took me ten years of active searching before I could make up my own mind, which I didn't know most of the time; how could I choose for another person?

Accumulated Wisdom

So with that out of the way, know that I am not going to tell you whom to marry. How, then, can I be of help? How can your parents and siblings and friends and church be of help? You need the advice and the perspective of others, but in the end you and you alone will choose your forever partner in life. So you need wisdom—a crash course in growing up and taming the horny instincts. Later, there will be plenty of time to turn the bull loose. Right now you need to build strong fences to keep the bull from mounting the first available heifer. And you need your mind and spirit free to walk in wisdom and objectivity, rather than be carried along on the currents of passion.

Call upon the accumulated wisdom of those who have gone before.

Though the final decision is yours, you don't have to do this all alone. You should welcome the opinions of those whom you respect. In all big decisions, you should call upon the accumulated wisdom of those who have gone before. " **. . . in the multitude of counsellors there is safety.**" Prov. 11:14 When you buy a house you consult the termite man, the title insurance companies, a builder; you talk to the neighbors, consider the building code, contact insurance companies; you research the risk of floods, traffic, availability of emergency medical services, fire, and police departments; you find out whether or not the house was formerly used as a meth lab, you make sure there is no black mold growing beneath the surface that could sicken your family, and, finally, you have the house tested for radon. Wow, all of that trouble and just for a house! Why not just do a quick drive-by and say, "Hey, that is a beautiful house; I would look good in it." With love at first site, what else matters?

He who aims too high may overshoot his target and not be able to retrieve his arrow.

One year after purchase, everything matters. A house you don't like, you can sell; wives are forever. Romans 7:2-3 In regard to marriage, you live in what you buy and it is your permanent address, like it or not—that is, if you are a follower of Jesus Christ. Impulse shopping is for shirts and pants, not forever partners. Choosing a wife takes a lot of thought, and I am going to try to help you think with the head on your shoulders, not the one in your pants.

Picky Parents

Parents are prone to expect their sons to marry the best. Having the benefit of years of experience, naturally they are going to be very selective and picky. Parents and friends are more likely to overlook your faults, but very clearly see the faults and shortcomings of the girls that interest you. Parents are ambitious where their children are concerned. Mom says, "No girl is too good for my son." You must be pretty special then. Great physique, drop-dead good looks, marathon runner, getting advanced degrees, already making a lot of money, extremely emotionally balanced, spiritually minded, and already showing promise to someday be of great service to mankind.

I can understand, then, why your parents and friends are so picky and demanding. They are not going to let you marry an ordinary girl, for you are no ordinary man.

He who aims too high may overshoot his target and not be able to retrieve his arrow.

Let's face it, 1% of men are special at the top; 1% are special needs at the bottom, and the rest of us are special only in our parents' eyes—or our own. In reality we are quite ordinary in more ways than our parents are willing to admit. I have known guys who let the good ones get away while they held out for a number 10. If your parents strain at a gnat, you may be left to marry a camel. Though most guys are 5s, their parents want them to marry 10s, not just in looks but in personality, spirituality, creativity, and so on. I am not suggesting that you settle for less than you value; just make sure it is your values you seek to fulfill and not someone else's.

In a Perfect World

In a perfect world . . . let me say it in a different way . . . in a world of normal Christianity, where young men walk after the Spirit of God and **"make not provision for the flesh, to fulfill the lusts thereof,"** Romans 13:14 and where parents are filled with the knowledge of the Lord, and neither parents nor children are possessed of worldly ambitions, I would say to the young men seeking brides, "Pray about it, seek the counsel of your parents, and follow God's leading." Occasionally I see this normal Christianity in action, but only in about 1% of the families.

A few of my readers have been in touch with God for years and live a life of relying on divine guidance. They don't particularly need this discussion on counsel. God has consistently led them in the small things; he will lead them in this big one—if they don't let their passions run away with them.

If your life has been marked by praying and receiving divine guidance, and you have a proven track record of divine illumination, then by all means humbly receive all counsel and then let God guide you, and you alone, to know his will.

The 99%

Most of my readers are nominal Christians at best and have never consciously experienced divine guidance. So what about this vast group of lackadaisical Christians whose parents have just barely hung on to their own marriages? Seldom does anyone pray and expect an answer, and the entire family cannot recount one miracle of answered prayer other than Grandma getting well after being hospitalized for three weeks. I would like to see this vast middle group of Christians start their marriages better paired than their parents.

This last generation of Christians has proven that "Christian" marriages are no better than those rooted in secularism. The young people are raised on Hollywood rather than the old wooden cross. Recreational dating and fornication have been the norm in the Christian church. Churches now have a very large "singles class," which is where divorcees go to find another spouse. The present situation has been alarming to church leaders and parents alike. So about twenty-five years ago, in reaction to this awful situation, ministers started developing betrothal/courtship methods designed to purify the process of coming to marriage. There was a

Your mind and spirit need to be free to walk in wisdom and objectivity rather than be carried along on the currents of passion.

need and the effort was noble, but, like all reactionary swings of the pendulum, it went too far and promised too much.

The wheat bread, homeschool movement has been fertile ground for these exotic betrothal and courtship systems. I am not talking about all betrothal or courtship, just some of the far-out patriarchal, medieval ideas of the "divine right" of the king/father figure. Father and mother get together with father and mother and arrange a marriage for son and daughter. I think they must have watched *Fiddler on the Roof* and thought it was biblical. I can't tell you how much tragedy and disappointment has come from that movement—even divorces.

Above all, pray like you have never prayed before.

When the system was young it produced great hope and excitement, but as many young people entered into somewhat of an arranged marriage, some of them discovered they were wed to someone they didn't even like. Mama liked him. Daddy said he was spiritual and had a good source of income, but the bride just found him to be a stranger with whom she had nothing in common.

I have received hundreds of sad letters from these betrothal arrangements. Not all is bad; there are some blessed stories as well, but when it goes wrong, the miserable sons and daughters blame their parents for their plight. It is one thing to make your own mistake. It is another thing for someone else to make it for you. When you make your own mistake, you accept the reality and try to make the most of it. When you are the victim of someone else's mistake you are likely to live in blame and bitterness.

In some of the very tightly controlled churches, they are adamant about their young people marrying within the denomination. Many of these churches have shrunk in numbers and there are not many prospective spouses available. Marrying within the church preserves the numbers. Sometimes the church is more concerned about perpetuating itself than about doing God's will.

Hear me when I say, there is no system or fixed chain of command that can prevent you from making a mistake in marriage.

God does not surrender his will to the dictates of mortal men. You are fallible. I am fallible. Your parents and pastor are fallible, and so is every matchmaker since Adam.

Children, Obey Your Parents

What about the verse, **"Children, obey your parents in the Lord: for this is right"**? Ephesians 6:1 If you are a child, then by all means, obey them. But then, children don't need help meets. They sit on the floor and color. Furthermore the passage qualifies the obedience as "in the Lord." If parents command you contrary to the Lord, then you are to do as Peter did when the government commanded him to stop preaching in Jesus' name. He said, **"We ought to obey God rather than men."** Acts 5:29 If you are old enough to be married, you are responsible for your own life and you are the one that will reap the results of any decisions you make or let others make for you. Blindly obeying does not make right a bad choice. You reap what you sow even if your daddy told you to sow it.

Daunting Indeed

If it all seems daunting to you, if you and those around you are too carnally focused to get divine leading and you have very little confidence in your ability to discover the will of God for yourself, there is still the tried and proven method of careful thought, wisdom, and good counsel. Above all, pray like you have never prayed before. Confess to God your ignorance and former carnality and ask him to open and shut doors. Keep the flesh under control and perhaps you can hear the voice of God like you never heard him before. Your life depends on it.

Wise Counsel

A wise man will hear, and will increase learning; and a man of understanding shall attain unto wise counsels: Proverbs 1:5

Beware ignoring counsel. **"My son, hear the instruction of thy father, and forsake not the law of thy mother."** Proverbs 1:8

You ask, "Are you for or against parental counsel in marriage?" I am for divine guidance and the best human wisdom available in choosing a help meet.

There is a real danger in blindly obeying parents or churches regarding whom you marry. Numbers 31:16; Proverbs 12:5 But there is also an equal or greater danger in ignoring or resisting parental advice and the counsel of others who care for you.

Seek the Counsel of Many

[I]n multitude of counsellers there is safety. Proverbs 24:6

"In multitude of counsellers…"? Why a multitude? Because all those who would give their counsel are fallible (including me) and will not be in agreement. I am not suggesting that you follow the consensus. The majority may be wrong as often as they are right, but hearing various perspectives enables us to think through our own mental and spiritual processes and analyze our motives. When you hear someone whose motives you do not respect agree with you, it should be alarming. If the devil or a known idiot takes your side, you will want to consider changing sides. On the other hand, if several people whom you respect share the same concern, you should be concerned as well and not act until you either come to agreement with them, or determine that they are motivated by unworthy considerations.

Truth will step forward in a way that is unmistakable.

When someone supposedly of the same faith and convictions as I disagrees with me, I cannot rest until I can clearly see which one of us is wrong and wherein lies the fallacy of thought. I dare not dismiss the concerns of a sincere person unless I can see that he is motivated by faulty logic or misled by personal hang-ups. Only then can I act without reserve. Be very careful (humble) when you turn your back on counsel, be it from parents or friends. The person most likely to be wrong is the one most involved emotionally. Guess who that is.

Counsel in the heart of man is like deep water; but a man of understanding will draw it out. Proverbs 20:5

The "drawing out" process is indeed a process. If your heart is right before God and you truly want his will, he will place his will in your heart, and through the counsel of others that wisdom will be drawn out of your heart to the surface where conscious thought resides. Truth is self-evident and often comes like the dawn, a little at a time until you stand in full light. Truth has a way of rising through the cloud of confusing opinions until it is the brightest thing in the sky. When you hear a dozen varied opinions supported by reason— some good, others not so good—truth will step forward in a way that is unmistakable. But only the humble and teachable and patient will discern truth from error. So listen to everyone who speaks—parents, pastors, counselors, friends, and even enemies—but only believe that which your spirit finds to be pure and lovely. Therein is the voice of God.

For what man knoweth the things of a man, save the spirit of man which is in him? even so the things of God knoweth no man, but the Spirit of God. 1 Corinthians 2:11

You will find the mind of God in your spirit, and an abundance of counsel often brings it to the surface.

If you feel ignorant and that you are likely to make a mistake, there is a passage you should memorize:

If any of you lack wisdom, let him ask of God, that giveth to all men liberally, and upbraideth not; and it shall be given him. James 1:5

God is more interested in you finding the right help meet than
you are. You don't take it as seriously as he does. He watches as 95%
of the young men make the wrong choice, and half of them end up
in divorce, while another 45% hang in there and suffer through it, or
discover God's way to a happy marriage
and give careful attention to fixing their
shortcomings. Many good marriages have
been constructed from the ashes of bad
ones, but why burn before you learn? Get
it right from the start and the two of you
can do something more with your lives
than struggle to achieve a good marriage.

*You will find the
mind of God in
your spirit, and
an abundance of
counsel often brings
it to the surface.*

Those men who have walked closest
to God will more likely be open to
counsel than will those men who have idled along
presumptuously, because they understand the wisdom in hearing
from other brothers.

A Warning

**A fool despiseth his father's instruction: but he that
regardeth reproof is prudent.** Proverbs 15:5

Some of my readers are fools (not my words; note the passage
above). You have heretofore been in bondage to your church and your
parents, and you celebrate the concept that you are now at liberty to
act independently of their counsel because you know they are not
spiritually minded and wise. You exalt yourself above all counsel and
latch on to that which justifies your foolishness. You have always
despised instruction and are likely to go on doing so. The fact that
your parents may not be wise and your church may be selfish, and
the grim truth that no one can tell you God's will for your life does
not mean that you can just do whatever you want and it will be

right. As your parents do not have a divine right to dictate to you the will of God, you have no right to expect God to bless your choices unless you choose what he has already chosen for you. There are many paths to ruin. Someone can choose it for you or you can choose it for yourself. Only divine wisdom can lead you in the way you should go. I wish I had words that could cause you to see the error in your thinking, but I do not.

> *The Bible is God's words, the most important words you will ever read. Read them.*

I would be tempted to do what many have done: to create a system of betrothal designed to save a fool from his folly, but then I and the people in control would be responsible for the outcome. I don't have enough faith in myself to make such an important choice for you.

I know this has sounded grim—downright scary. But if you could read for just one month the letters I receive, you would lose your self-confidence and your confidence in any system or person to choose your perfect help meet. I can give you a thousand testimonies of marvelous success but they do not diminish the many tragedies. It is my heart to save you now rather than having to write a book to you later, trying to put Humpty-Dumpty back together again.

Don't go away discouraged—the book is not over. There are bright things to come. Hope is in the air. All things are possible in Christ.

A Warning Against Hormones

Hormonally driven guys can "fall in love" with a girl just by seeing her picture. That is like prospecting for gold and the first hole you fall into you stake your claim, call it a gold mine, and start digging. Good feelings and great passion do not mean there is compatibility. And when a guy gets the hots for a girl, he will not

Hormonally driven guys can "fall in love" with a girl just by seeing her picture.

welcome negative criticism. He is sure pure bliss awaits him in her lovely arms. "How could anything that feels so good be wrong? We were made for each other." I've news for you: all girls are made for all guys. It is a simple matter of plumbing and hormones waiting for opportunity.

I have seen a hottie walk into a room and watched every man there "fall in love." If you are searching for a help meet and you don't distrust yourself, you are a self-inflicted tragedy planning your own demise.

I know that sounds cold and cynical to you young and romantic guys who are swept along by storybook idealism, but there will come a time when you are too "in love" (horny) to listen to your own brain, much less to your parents or friends. Don't wait until the heat of battle to prepare defenses against your brainless flesh. Determine right now not to believe your body and your romantic emotions when you are swept into a vortex of passion and desire. Determine to rely only on your reason. Set some rules for yourself before you feel the heat.

I can't help but think I am wasting my time and good paper on most of you guys. Once a tree starts falling it is too late to decide where you want it to land. You must save yourself; no one else can. Most of you have parents who understand what I am saying, though they may not be able to frame it in words. That is why they get so frustrated and crazy with many of your decisions. They see you soaked in flammables and looking for a flame to warm yourself.

If any of you lack wisdom, let him ask of God.

Time to Consider:

There are 31 chapters in the book of Proverbs—an easy read of one chapter a day for each month. Chapters 1–9 contain a fatherly exhortation to young men. Chapters 10–24 show the contrast between wisdom and foolishness. The last chapter is written by a mother telling her son what to look for in choosing a bride. Twenty-two times in the book of Proverbs an appeal is made to young men by saying, "My son."

For the word of God is quick, and powerful, and sharper than any twoedged sword, piercing even to the dividing asunder of soul and spirit, and of the joints and marrow, and is a discerner of the thoughts and intents of the heart.
Hebrews 4:12

God speaks of his written Word as quick (alive), powerful, sharper than any two-edged sword. God's Word is effectual; it is able to make you wise as you read, study, and believe it.

Begin a notebook on the book of Proverbs. Choose verses to memorize from each chapter every day as you read through it each month. Soon you will have much of God's instruction written on your heart as you read and record what you are learning.

Start every day with this request: "God, I ask for wisdom and knowledge to seek and know you."

If any of you lack wisdom, let him ask of God, that giveth to all men liberally, and upbraideth not; and it shall be given him. James 1:5

Did a girl exist
who would want
to marry a
missionary?

Chapter 3

LONG-DISTANCE BRIDE

This is the story of a young man who had considerable help in finding the love of his life. From his youth Joshua had sought the Lord and walked in truth. God has richly rewarded him. It took divine intervention to find the lady of choice. God does that on occasion. Here is Joshua and Kelsie's love story in his own words.

Three Strikes and You're Out?

I was 24 years old, and as the year 2003 was drawing to a close, I had reached the grim conclusion that God probably didn't want me to be married any time soon. While my life heretofore had seen many successes, romance had not been among them. Onlookers, perhaps, suspected that I just was not trying hard enough, but this was far from true.

Like any normal young man, I wanted to be married. Badly. I had wanted it since I was eight. My difficulties were of a more practical nature. Did a girl exist who would want to marry a missionary, and, if so, how was I to find her? Already I had made three attempts at courtship that had fizzled before they ever got off the ground. I'll not provide details here, but don't worry: my stories were devoid of drama. Mostly, they came down to the fact that the girl in question simply did not like me.

This string of failures was a relatively new experience for me. Since my early teenage years I had committed my life wholly to

God, and I had seen Him graciously bless and advance me in many miraculous ways. I had learned to discern His provision and guidance,

> *Over the years of seeking God, reading his Word, and honoring him with my life, I had learned to discern His provision and guidance.*

usually proceeding with confidence in the knowledge that He was with me.

Thus, after my third strike at beginning a relationship, I began to suspect that I was missing some sort of divine memo. My utter failure to progress in my attempts at finding a life partner led me to a growing fear that God did not want me to get married. At least not now. But if not now, when? For some reason, the ten-year figure popped into my head, and was subsequently expelled as quickly as it had arrived. Surely God did not intend for me to press on alone! Yet seemingly, the handwriting had appeared on the wall, and there was not much I could do to remove it.

At last I gave up trying. I was tired. I was distracted from my work. The emotional ups and downs of courtship-on/courtship-off had left me discouraged. At this point I made a decision that I believe the Lord is looking for in all his children, especially the single ones who are seeking a mate: I decided to wait on God. And by waiting, I don't mean that lethargic inactivity wherein the proverbial farmer prays for potatoes without the willingness to pick up the hoe. Folks, I had hoed my very best. I had fulfilled every requirement I knew of. And after praying, searching, talking to fathers, seeking counsel, praying more, and wishing desperately to find a wife, all I got from God was silence. But I had learned that divine silence is itself an answer. "Wait. My time is not yet. Trust me." And so I waited.

In a way, I felt that I had fewer answers than when I had begun. There were many things I did not understand, many courtship and marriage questions that remained a mystery. But I did know one thing: God is faithful. Marriage or no marriage, I had committed my life to following him, and that was not about to change.

A few weeks later, I received an email from my sister Jennifer, who wrote, "I recently shared a room with a wonderful young lady named Kelsie…"

First Things First

My introduction to Kelsie was unlike anything I had previously imagined. When first I heard of her, we were about as far apart geographically as it is possible for any two people to be on this planet. In early 2004, she was living in Oklahoma with her parents while I was working on a short-term mission project in Thailand.

My sister's email description of Kelsie was glowing. The highlights included such demonstratives as "godly, virtuous, and committed," and a particular one that caught my attention: "praying to marry a missionary." This last point addressed a major question that I had pondered for some time: what type of girl would consent to marry a missionary, knowing that she would likely spend the rest of her life in some remote country overseas? Apparently, this Kelsie was just such a girl.

Marriage or no marriage, I had committed my life to following him, and that was not about to change.

Further inquiry revealed that not only was Kelsie praying to marry a missionary, she had been on many mission trips herself. She had served in Taiwan and Mexico, and she was fluent in Spanish.

Due to a long-standing personal conviction, I knew that my next step was to contact Kelsie's father, Danny. To me, it was imperative that this be accomplished without Kelsie's knowledge. In case things did not work out, I wanted to be able to make a quiet exit without damaging her emotionally.

But there was a practical problem: I did not have the ability to make outgoing calls on my phone from Thailand. As I discussed the matter with my parents via email, we determined that the best solution would be for my father to contact Kelsie's father.

Although I do not have a transcript of that conversation, I do remember experiencing a measure of concern as I imagined it in advance. The major components which I foresaw went something like this:

My father picks up the receiver, dials the number for the Powell household. The phone rings, and a man answers.

"Hello?"

"Yes, may I speak with Danny Powell please?"

"This is Danny."

"Hi Danny, my name is Mike Steele. You don't know me, and I don't know you, but my daughter Jennifer has met your daughter Kelsie. Anyway, I'm actually calling on behalf of my son Joshua. You don't know him either. He's a missionary to Ukraine, but he's currently working in Thailand. He's interested in beginning a relationship with your daughter Kelsie, whom he also doesn't know. He wanted to contact you about this without Kelsie knowing, but he can't make calls out of Thailand. But he can email. He would like to know if he can send you an email about starting a relationship with Kelsie."

Due to a long-standing personal conviction, I knew my next step was to contact her dad.

I imagined silence, and then "click."

Who was I kidding? What father in his right mind would even listen to such an absurd request? Despite my wavering faith, it turns out God was moving after all. Danny was very much in his right mind, and he was very willing to listen. After the two fathers got off the phone, I received the go-ahead to send my introductory email.

Scarcely able to believe that this was all happening, I composed a simple message in which I introduced myself, gave a very brief explanation of my work as a missionary, and expressed my desire to "get to know Kelsie in a courtship relationship with the goal of marriage in mind should the Lord so direct." I stressed my respect for the fact that Kelsie was his daughter, that he was her God-ordained head, and that I was ready to proceed in whatever way and at whatever pace he desired. Then I hit send, and waited.

A positive reply arrived soon thereafter, and Danny and I began our correspondence.

Dating the Dad?

In our modern culture, many Christian young men scoff at the idea of contacting a girl's father before pursuing a relationship with her. "After all, she is an adult. Let her make her own decision." While I realize that there may be exceptions, my position to this day remains the same: if at all possible, ask Dad first. The benefits of such an approach are numerous, and in my case, though a bit nervous initially, I never regretted for a moment my decision to correspond with Kelsie's father before making my intentions known to her.

When Danny and I began emailing, I had no idea what to expect. But I knew that for now, Kelsie was under his jurisdiction, and if I wanted a chance at winning her heart, I first needed to obtain Danny's permission. I invited him to proceed at his own pace, to ask whatever questions he wanted, and to take whatever steps he felt were necessary in order to assure himself that I was ready and able to love, lead, and provide for his daughter in marriage.

Our early emails were largely composed of basic facts about our two families. He asked many questions about my upbringing and my ministry. In turn he also told me a lot about their family. Far from the extended grilling I had feared, I found that Danny and I actually got along quite well. He was very positive and encouraging. As I would later learn, Danny had felt strongly for a couple of months that God was about to bring Kelsie's life partner onto the scene, and he had been waiting. From the time he read my first email, he strongly sensed that this courtship was God's design.

I think it is no coincidence that of all the players in this particular courtship drama, it was Kelsie's father who was the first to be convinced in his heart that this was a marriage made in heaven. Before I even knew the name Kelsie Powell, God had impressed upon Danny that the time was near.

Let's Tell Kelsie

After only three weeks, Danny surprised me by stating that he felt this was of the Lord and that we should tell Kelsie about it. "How would you like to tell her?" he asked. Since I was still in Thailand, my options were limited. Ultimately, we decided that I would write an introductory letter. Danny and his wife, Cindy, would print it on parchment paper, tie it up with a burgundy ribbon, and present it to Kelsie.

I believe at the time there were those who, upon hearing our story, worried that Danny and I were concocting an arranged marriage in which Kelsie had no say. Nothing could be further from the truth. As her father, Danny was merely doing what any wise father should do: protecting his daughter from potentially harmful relationships and doing all he could to find for her the man who would become her lifelong companion. That said, it was understood from the beginning that Kelsie had veto power. I had proposed a courtship, Danny had approved, but the final decision would be Kelsie's.

This was not an arranged marriage. Kelsie had the final say.

At the time all this was transpiring, Kelsie was away teaching at a girls' retreat. Her parents made their preparations in her absence, and on the day she returned, Danny suggested the family go on an after-dinner stroll in a local park. As Kelsie's younger brother entertained himself by tossing stones into a nearby pond, she and her parents chatted.

"Kelsie, I have a new foreign language that I think you should learn," Danny remarked.

"Really?" asked Kelsie, intrigued. In the Powell family, this was not an unusual request. Congruent with her desire to work in foreign missions, Kelsie had mastered Spanish and conversational Chinese, and had lately been studying French.

> *We were thousands of miles apart, yet God used our apparent limitations as a means of strengthening our relationship.*

Danny continued, "Yes, I think you might be interested in learning Ukrainian."

With that, he handed her a small, worn, paperback Ukrainian phrasebook. Opening it, she immediately noticed a name penned inside the front cover: Joshua Steele.

The Beginning

I am told that most young ladies receive a pleasant sort of shock when they learn of a secret admirer. Kelsie was no exception. She, too, had experienced some disappointments before meeting me and had wondered if a man of godly character would ever pursue her.

Now, as her father handed over the rolled parchment, she loosened the ribbon and read my invitation.

> *Dear Kelsie,*
>
> *Although you do not know me, I have been corresponding with your parents for the past month or so in regards to a possible courtship with you. I have really enjoyed getting to know them, and in a way getting to know you through them…*

...we have been "talking about you" for some time now, and your mother and father wrote me recently, saying that they felt this would be a good time to let you know about all of this.

And so my purpose in writing you this letter is to see if you would be willing to begin a courtship relationship, with the goal of marriage in mind should the Lord so direct us.

Kelsie's immediate response was to get alone and pray. She had my letter, the Ukrainian phrasebook, and a stack of missionary newsletters that I had written over the past two and a half years.

As Kelsie prayed, the rest of us held our breaths and waited. Happily, we did not have to wait long. A few hours later I received Kelsie's response in which she excitedly agreed to begin a relationship!

Mystery Courtship

As Kelsie and I embarked on what would become a lifelong journey together, our relationship was unlike anything I had envisioned. I was still in Thailand and she in Oklahoma. My acquaintance with her family had reached the ripe old age of three weeks, and neither of us had ever seen the other in person. Our budding new friendship sounded more like a success story from an online dating site than a Christian courtship. Yet none involved could deny that God was leading.

Let me clarify at this point what exactly we had begun. Neither of us had agreed to marriage. How could we? We knew only the barest facts about each other and were proceeding primarily based on the sincere belief that this was God's direction.

Our approach was practical. Separated by thousands of miles, we focused on exchanging information and seeking to confirm that this was, in fact, God's will. It was understood that both of us were free to back out at any time if we did not believe God was leading us to proceed.

Unlike most young people entering courtship, we could not meet face-to-face and so relied heavily on written correspondence. Looking back, both of us have observed that God used this apparent limitation as a means of maturing and strengthening our relationship. As we wrote, we discussed a variety of issues including our views on children, finances, the family in general, church, ministry, education, and employment. Woven into these fact exchanges were plenty of personal details and the simple, excited chatter of two young people who are rapidly falling in love.

I asked her to marry me, and she joyfully agreed.

But *love* was one word I refrained from using at the beginning. Too many have cheapened that word by applying it early and often to anything and anyone who happens to catch their fancy. I wanted Kelsie to know that when first I confessed my love for her, it would be more than just words.

I Love You!

It wasn't long before I knew I needed to get Stateside. Only a couple of weeks after completing a transition back to Ukraine from Thailand, I flew home to Texas where Kelsie was waiting for me. Her parents had moved up to Calgary, Canada, due to a work assignment from Danny's employer, but Kelsie stayed behind so we could meet and begin to spend time together in person.

As the days passed, my confidence in our relationship grew steadily. Soon I decided that it was time to tell Kelsie in no uncertain terms that I loved her. Trained as I was to treat such steps with extreme caution, I decided to check with Danny first. I sent off an email and soon received his reply. He gave his permission excitedly and even expressed some surprise that I had not already told Kelsie of my love!

Armed with this approval, I purchased a dozen red roses and placed them in the parlor of my grandmother's house where Kelsie had been staying. That afternoon, Kelsie and I entered the parlor together, where she immediately saw the flowers. Her face beamed as she noticed the card protruding from the side. Inscribed on it in large letters were the words: "I love you, Princess Kelsie!"

A few days later, I asked Kelsie to marry me, and she joyfully agreed. Perhaps no two people on earth were happier that day than we were. After long months of waiting, seeking, praying, and trusting God, we knew for certain that each of us had found our life partner in the other.

The days and weeks that followed were a delightful blend of travel, meeting family, wedding planning, and of course, spending every possible moment with each other. On September 18, 2004, our young courtship officially ended as we crossed the threshold from singleness into marriage. Less than a month later, we arrived in Ukraine and began building our new life together.

Ever After

At the time of this writing, Kelsie and I have been married for over eight years, and the Lord has blessed us with three precious children who are the joy of our lives. While married life has certainly presented its challenges, we have faced them together: not as competitors, but as friends. In fact, the phrase "you're my best friend" is one used often in our home.

We count ourselves very blessed to have had parents and mentors who urged us to trust God in the area of marriage, and we can testify along with many thousands of saints that God is indeed faithful to direct the paths of those who wait on him.

*Trust in the LORD
with all thine heart; and lean not
unto thine own understanding.
In all thy ways
acknowledge him, and he shall
direct thy paths.*

Proverbs 3:5-6

48

TIME TO CONSIDER:

Proverbs 2:1–11 says:

My son, if thou wilt...

1. receive my words, and
2. hide my commandments with thee;
3. So that thou incline thine ear unto wisdom, and
4. apply thine heart to understanding;
5. Yea, if thou criest after knowledge, and
6. liftest up thy voice for understanding;
7. If thou seekest her as silver, and
8. searchest for her as for hid treasures;

Then shalt thou...

1. understand the fear of the LORD, and
2. find the knowledge of God.
3. For the LORD giveth wisdom:
4. out of his mouth cometh knowledge and understanding.
5. He layeth up sound wisdom for the righteous:
6. he is a buckler to them that walk uprightly.
7. He keepeth the paths of judgment, and
8. preserveth the way of his saints.
9. Then shalt thou understand righteousness, and
8. judgment, and
9. equity; yea,
10. every good path.

When wisdom entereth into thine heart, and knowledge is pleasant unto thy soul; Discretion shall preserve thee, understanding shall keep thee:

Make an outline of this passage in your Proverbs notebook.

Our actions and reactions do indeed reap results in this present life as well as in eternity.

*Every good gift and every
perfect gift is from above, and
cometh down from the Father
of lights, with whom is no
variableness, neither
shadow of turning.*

James 1:17

Chapter 4

HOW DO YOU KNOW SHE IS THE ONE?

I know that in the modern Christian church there are movements toward formal courtship supposedly based on biblical models. Many of these lately designed movements do not allow a guy and gal to get to know each other without first making a commitment to marriage. You might say to a father, "What do you say if I join your family this Saturday when you go to the zoo?"

He might respond, "What are your intentions toward my daughter?"

You might answer, "I intend to get to know her as a friend in the context of your family."

He might respond, "You will need to correspond with me for one year before you can speak to her; I don't want you to trifle with my daughter's heart."

"Forget it; sorry I asked; I don't buy anything without looking at the merchandise," you answer.

Do not allow yourself to be drawn into a situation where you must commit to anything other than virtue and respect before you thoroughly know a gal. You should not become romantic or even flirty with a girl unless you are publicly committed to marriage, but it is possible to get to know many young ladies as friends with nothing more implied. Don't toy with a girl's heart—no recreational dating—but don't allow anyone to toy with your heart by asking you to commit to buy the merchandise when all you have done is viewed it through the store window. You haven't asked to try it on; you just want to view it before making a lifetime commitment. It might not fit you at all.

Keep It Pure

The world thinks the best way to shop for pajamas is to sleep in them a few times until you know how they feel; then you buy the one that is most comfortable. The problem is that we are much more than mating animals. We are complex, living souls with a single gift of virtue that can only be spent one time. It should be kept sacred until you give it to someone who will treasure it and guard it the rest of their life. Coming to marriage without your virtue is like coming to a birthday party with your balloon already busted, your candle already burnt, and your present already unwrapped and soiled with use—an anticlimax at the least, and a big show of disrespect for the birthday girl. She will always know she ended up with seconds—leftovers. She will never feel that special something so precious to a young bride.

Christians have a commitment to maintain their virtue until marriage.

Christians have a commitment to maintain their virtue until marriage. We don't screw around and test the waters. But, to our shame, there is less commitment to keep the heart in a state of virginity as well as the body. Romantic dating is releasing the dog on a short chain. It is emotional fornication. When you are infatuated with a girl and want to be near her, to smell her, touch her ever so innocently, to look in her eyes and say sweet things, you are doing 90% of what married couples do. We call it foreplay. It is the getting-ready stage of sexual intercourse. It is the art of arousal and is meant to naturally lead to copulation.

When you get romantically involved with a girl, you are tasting the sweet fruit but not swallowing. It gives new meaning to the word frustration. It feels good because it is what a man was made for—one man and one woman until death do they part.

Think about it. If you were married and your wife were to have a male friend with whom she cavorted as you now do with your girlfriend, would you consider her to be unfaithful to you, committing adultery, or on the verge of it? Of course! You would consider it to be a betrayal of your vows. Why? Because you know

Tasting but not swallowing gives new meaning to the word frustration.

she would be giving away something precious that belongs to her husband alone. How, then, do you now justify taking what is not yours? Do her romantic gestures not belong to her future husband as much now as they will then? You are consuming her virtue for the feel-good sensations of sexual foreplay that should be reserved for her husband alone.

Let's look at it another way. If you discovered your father relating to the young girl as do you, would you accuse him of inappropriate behavior? Again, would her father consider your behavior inappropriate—sinful? Does God consider it sinful? People don't conceal the high and holy, only the low and shameful.

Keep thy heart with all diligence; for out of it are the issues of life. Put away from thee a froward mouth, and perverse lips put far from thee. Let thine eyes look right on, and let thine eyelids look straight before thee. Ponder the path of thy feet, and let all thy ways be established. Turn not to the right hand nor to the left: remove thy foot from evil. Proverbs 4: 23-27

The betrothal and courtship doctrines were born and have gained traction as a reaction to the culture of Christian dating and fornication. They may be too regulated and a bit overmuch sometimes, actually preventing many young girls from having any suitors, but they have correctly defined the problem and offered a solution even if it is often legalistic and rigid.

How do you feel about some horny young man out there right now romantically involved with your future wife whom you have not yet met? Are you indifferent to the fact that he is engaging in emotional and maybe sexual foreplay with your someday wife? How is she going to feel when he moves on to give another girl a spin, still searching for his sexual partner, but in the mean time, enjoying toying with emotional fornication? Tell me, no, tell yourself, are you okay with their foolery? What makes your foolery the exception?

> *If you are a Christian indeed, a disciple of Jesus Christ, you have a desire to be holy in body and soul, and you would never want to bring harm to a young lady, the future wife of some young man.*

If you are a Christian indeed, a disciple of Jesus Christ, you have a desire to be holy in body and soul, and you would never want to bring harm to a young lady, the future wife of some young man. So in the process of getting to know many young ladies in anticipation of discovering one to be your suited helper, do not sacrifice your virtue—or the girl's—on the altar of temporary pleasure. Romantic dating is totally inappropriate until you have made a public commitment to marriage and are close to the marriage—no more than a few weeks. And all foreplay is unacceptable until you are free to play the game to the end.

So when you are getting to know girls, keep your emotional distance until you have made a commitment to one special girl.

If we could turn off our romantic needs until we got to know a gal it would make things much simpler, but we are built to need a woman, and it is so tempting to become personal. Even when there is an absolute commitment to moral purity, there is still the temptation to intimately confide, to share one's deep feelings, to buddy up, just the two of us, to care as a man cares for a woman. It can be a touch-free relationship, but it quickly becomes romantically satisfying while building in frustration. It is this very magnetism that prompts us all to seek marriage. But you must know where your fire burns and what fuels it. You must avoid intimacy while getting to know girls as people instead of romantic partners.

How Can I Know?

You might ask, "How can I know that we are going to be compatible? There is only one way and that is to get to know any prospective spouse by spending time talking and doing things together. Consult her friends. Become acquainted with her social circle. Obviously, when you are part of a large community of folk who grow up together, you will know many girls very well. You will have played sports with them, gone on picnics and church outings, gone shopping together, and then, as you get older, young people go out to eat or go to concerts or public events together, maybe participate in local elections, and many other events that put young people in proximity to one another.

Working together cutting firewood or helping build a mission compound is a good way to get to know a girl.

The most natural context for this kind of socialization is community life where people work and play together without any romance. If you are not part of a community where you are raised around girls then you must seek social contexts where the focus is not on boy/girl coupling but on some outside common interest that provides a reason for you to be together, such as a large number of young adults playing sports, singing in a choir, practicing musical instruments, visiting the sick and helping the poor, and going on short-term mission trips.

In a social context that has a purpose other than dating, both the guys and girls can relax and pretend to not take any special notice of anyone in particular. A guy can talk to a girl without either of them thinking it means anything at all. A guy can stop talking to one girl and start talking to another without anyone getting their feelings hurt. A girl can even approach a guy in total relaxation and start up a conversation. There is no promise and no expectation and, with all the people around, no chance for getting personal. It is that very lack of personal intimacy that leaves the door open to get to know many people. Churches have camps, the Amish have work days, and there are mission conferences where young men can go to meet godly girls. A young man should take the opportunity to go places where young women are.

Getting to Know You...Long Distance

It is easy to get to know a person when you are both part of a community, but in our modern world that is not always possible. You need to go shopping where you are most likely to find the kind of girl you hope to marry. If you want a mall girl who spends her days hanging out with the girls, giggling at the mall, then go to the mall to shop; but if you want a godly gal who is serious about life, one who will homeschool your children and prepare healthy meals, who will dedicate her life wholly to blessing you and ministering to her children, then you will need to go where girls of that caliber are located.

You may have to put up with some overprotective daddies and some scrutinizing mamas, but remember, the treasure you seek has been preserved in her virginity and training by those very over-protective parents. It is usually worth the hassle. And there are a lot of reasonable parents who do not want to dissect your soul or do a brain scan on you. They just want to know that you are for real and that you are a serious suitor, not just a horny hound looking for a good time. Daddy will want to know if you have been viewing pornography and if you are holding down a job. He will want to know if you are emotionally stable and assure himself that you are not a radical, fringe nut job. Most homeschool parents have trained their daughters to be wise and will trust them to make their own decisions about marriage, so go for the gold and find one of those delightful beauties as pure as cherub wings, ready to love her man to the end.

I am not in the loop, so I don't know where they congregate, but I am sure there are homeschool events and gatherings that will provide you with a parade of possible mates. Seek out the churches were several righteous families attend. Sometimes you can happen upon a home church with half a dozen families, each with eight or ten kids—enough eligible girls to make a young man tremble with excitement. Start attending and get to know the families.

I know many fine young ladies who are hidden treasures. Go treasure hunting.

Do not hesitate to boldly enquire when you spot a lovely young lady in the presence of her family. Walk up and introduce yourself right in a restaurant or grocery store. Discuss common interests, and as the door opens, offer to come visit them and help the father or brothers do some job— repair the roof, clean the swimming pool, paint the house—anything that will allow them to observe you and you to observe the sisters. Sure, they will know what you are up to, but the soft approach makes it easier on everybody, and they are likely to appreciate the lack of intensity. I know many fine—very fine—young ladies who have never been approached. They are hidden treasures. Go treasure hunting.

What if she is from a different state and you have never been around her before? There is nothing so revealing as taking a supervised missionary trip together. Spend two weeks with a group in the tropics, with heat and rain and bug bites and lack of proper hygiene, with poor food and frustrations and disappointments and sleeplessness, early mornings and late evenings, and you will know her very well. Everything comes out.

Spend the day with her family on an outing—a long, tiresome day with brothers and sisters around. You need to see her after her defenses are down. Anyone can pretend for a few hours, but time and trials have a way of reducing us to reality where the soul emerges into full light. Watch her. If she is impatient with her brothers and sisters, she will be impatient with you. If she disrespects her father, she will disrespect you. If she whines, she is a whiner.

You may decide you can live with the whining or the disrespect because it is the best you can do. You are no great catch yourself. Well, at least you know what you are getting into, and you will be prepared to put up with her imperfections. I am sure she will be putting up with a lot of crummy stuff from you. Birds of a feather, you know.

You can look for a perfect wife; I did, but then I married a human girl not yet mature or complete. Yet she was my pick among a thousand.

I was going for the gold.

If we keep our eyes open and think without the blindfold of emotional entanglement, there will come a time when some girl satisfies most of our expectations and we find we just can't live without her. That is what it usually comes down to. The most objective wisdom will guide the average fellow just so long, and then one day he falls for a gal and is blinded until he has been married about two weeks. Start out being cautious, using your head, and you may make a decision based on wisdom instead of pure animal attraction.

No Greater Joy Ministries (nogreaterjoy.org) has what we call Shindigs. They are gatherings for families and singles to get together for four days of meeting, preaching, teaching, visiting, sports, and music. The Shindigs are fertile grounds for getting to know someone with the possibility of marriage. Here is the story of one such couple meeting at the last Shindig.

It Was Like I Always Knew Her

At thirty-two years old I am ready to get married. I have my education, a good job, and a constant yearning for a wife, but finding a possible spouse has proved futile. I don't live in a godly Central Park where girls jog by every few minutes. It is more like the remote mountains of Montana where only cows and cowboys range. At our tiny local church the only available lady is a 75-year-old widow. She's cute but a little too old. Several families have contacted my family seeking for me to come and meet their daughter, but I just don't like being set up. I wanted to do my own hunting.

Over the years I have walked in truth and honored God. It has not been easy, as I have the same male disposition as the rest of mankind. It is important to me that my future wife come to marriage having followed the Lord in purity. This has also limited my selection of a bride, but I have been willing to wait. But lately I have felt my waiting days are over.

At first I thought the Shindig was a weird idea, but after considering the possibility of hundreds of like-minded females all under the same roof, I changed my mind. I didn't admit, even to myself, that I was going wife hunting, but I knew I didn't want to live alone the rest of my life. Even the word alone has a bad ring to it. The Shindig was packed with at least 1500 people and there were more beautiful girls there than I had ever seen in one place. I heard a guy say it was like dying and going to Muslim heaven . . . almost.

There were a lot of unmarried men checking out the ladies, so I had serious competition. Since there were so many females and there was so little time, I decided to cut some corners and go for the gold. I am a practical guy.

When I first got there I went straight up to meet some of the leaders and missionaries in order to establish a working friendship. I wanted a lead on the best girls there. I knew it would be easy to get swept up with the first cute girl that smiled and giggled at me, and I didn't want that to happen.

Right off I noticed one of the girls who was volunteering to help set up the stage. She seemed cheerful, more mature than some of the teenyboppers, and when I had a chance to speak to her she just seemed comfortable to be around, like I had known her a long time.

With a girl in mind, it really sharpened my senses to what it would be like to have a woman—that woman—in my life.

The second day, I asked some of the leaders if they knew her and what they thought. Everyone had glowing reports. Over the next few days I had several opportunities to talk with her while in a group but never alone except for a minute here or there. She had jumped into the program, so she was really busy helping. I don't think she ever knew I was checking her out.

The last day I stopped one of the married couples and asked right out, "What girl do you think is the best catch of the whole Shindig?" They both looked around the large room until their eyes settled on a girl. "Her," they said without hesitation, and it was the gal who had caught my eye. I made sure I had her email address before I left for home.

I prayed about getting in touch with her and spent a lot of time thinking about what I wanted in a wife. With a girl in mind, it really sharpened my senses to what it would be like to have a woman—that woman—in my life. After a week or so I emailed her and asked if she would be open to emailing back and forth, and I told her I would be glad to contact her dad before I proceeded. She wrote back and said she had talked to her dad and showed him my email. He said he wasn't interested in courting me; it wasn't their style. He told her that she had proven herself to walk before the Lord in truth and he knew she would be wise. I was surprised, since I had always assumed the dad would put me through the grill. It was nice not being roasted.

We started writing and asking serious questions of each other. After a few weeks I told her I wanted to talk on the phone. She hesitated a little, but I pushed. We have covered a lot of weighty life issues. It has been a good way of really getting to know someone well without being put to the test physically. What made it better was that we had already met, so I wasn't staring into an empty mirror and wondering. I think being able to meet someone, even briefly, is really good because if the chemistry is not there, then it will save everyone a lot of trouble and time. BUT, for me at least, the chemistry was brewing. Our relationship is growing as we talk through every issue that comes to our minds. It is amazing how much we think alike, with all the same goals for life, children, ministry, doctrine, and convictions. The time writing has given both of us a chance to pray and seek God's wisdom, and it has caused me to pine for the time we can be together. We still have some getting to know each other to cover, but it is happening fast. It has only been a few months, but I can see how the wind is blowing and expect a warm spring. Just thinking about her makes me sweat.

Our relationship is growing as we talk through every issue that comes to our minds.

Just sign me,
Almost…

62

TIME TO CONSIDER:

Trust in the LORD with all thine heart; and lean not unto thine own understanding. In all thy ways acknowledge him, and he shall direct thy paths.

Be not wise in thine own eyes: fear the LORD, and depart from evil. It shall be health to thy navel, and marrow to thy bones. Honour the LORD with thy substance, and with the firstfruits of all thine increase: So shall thy barns be filled with plenty, and thy presses shall burst out with new wine.

Happy is the man that findeth wisdom, and the man that getteth understanding. For the merchandise of it is better than the merchandise of silver, and the gain thereof than fine gold. She is more precious than rubies: and all the things thou canst desire are not to be compared unto her.

Length of days is in her right hand; and in her left hand riches and honour. Her ways are ways of pleasantness, and all her paths are peace. She is a tree of life to them that lay hold upon her: and happy is every one that retaineth her.

The LORD by wisdom hath founded the earth; by understanding hath he established the heavens. By his knowledge the depths are broken up, and the clouds drop down the dew.

**My son, let not them depart from thine eyes: keep sound
wisdom and discretion: So shall they be life unto thy soul,
and grace to thy neck. Then shalt thou walk in thy way
safely, and thy foot shall not stumble.**

(Selections from Proverbs 3)

Add to your Proverbs notebook ideas you learned from this story.

---

*Happy is the man that findeth
wisdom, and the man that
getteth understanding.*
Proverbs 3:13

---

*The longer I live, the
clearer it is that a man is
just not all there until he
has his wife.*

Chapter 5

MY NEAR-FATAL MISTAKE

Before we continue with our study, I want to tell you the story of how I almost made a fatal mistake.

How You KNOW She's Not the ONE

It is with great reluctance, almost shame, that I admit here in print that there was a time in my youth when I wore a suit and tie and kept my thick, black hair slicked back like a good 50s and 60s Southern Baptist preacher. My excuse is that I was young, and when you are young you tend to do silly stuff to gain acceptance.

I was created to preach, teach, and write the gospel. From the time I first stood and preached to a bunch of drunks at Calvary Rescue Mission in Memphis, Tennessee, I have loved preaching the gospel. In my church, the monkey suit went with the position. I would have worn pink leotards and a superman cape if they were required. There were several of us preacher boys back then, so we all took turns preaching on Sunday evenings, and, of course, I was at Calvary Mission or Memphis Union Mission preaching to the drunks every chance I had, which was usually several times a week. I soon discovered that the young Navy men walking the streets made a great fishing hole, so I shared the gospel with them as well.

Oh, but I loved being invited to new churches to preach because it was a new crowd and I could check out all the lovely ladies for a possible bride. (Take note men: going to new churches is a great way of meeting prospects.) I am not being prideful; preachers do have a real appeal to the ladies, and I was handsome to boot, especially in a three-piece suit, okra-colored shirt, and purple tie. At least I thought those colors looked good.

Scouting for females was a very earnest endeavor for me. There was this unwritten list tucked away in my brain as I looked over each herd of beautiful possibilities. She must be a beauty—that was a given. It was simply a part of my male needs. It would be good if she could sing and play the piano, since I was a preacher and all meetings need a little music. Yes, music was good. I much preferred slender girls, although, as I have aged, I can't remember why skinny was so appealing; there is much less to love on when you marry a skinny gal, but that is another story that I'll save for the sex chapter in the married men's book.

Some things have to be done right the first time, and marriage is one.

Let's see, back to my unwritten list of prerequisites in women . . . I thought girls with presence and dignity were really cool. This type of girl would make a good preacher's wife, at least at the time it seemed so. My gal had to have long hair, although I did take a few short-haired girls out to eat after an evening meeting. I figured hair does grow, and the girls I took out to eat were so fine.

No matter how beautiful she was, I never gave a girl any further thought if I detected that she might be moody, lazy, or uninterested in ministry. I knew which way I was headed, and the only girls that interested me were already clearly headed in that direction. Life—married life in particular—is trying enough without having to pull a lazy, emotionally demanding or lost woman around, hoping for her to change. No, I wasn't stupid even in the days when I wore suits and ties and had a daily shave.

When I was a young man, our church youth were always getting together to sing or witness or for some group sports event. It was a wholesome opportunity I readily took advantage of. All these outings allowed me to watch the local girls so I could see if any of them walked the edge of dishonor in how they dressed or conducted themselves. I took notice of whether they were dishonoring to their parents or had any signs of a pouty spirit. More than half the girls in the youth group were quickly put on the "NO" list. I also noticed the girls who were always ready to help do different odd jobs at church, which indicated a physically healthy, emotionally sound, and spiritually giving person. Things like this impressed me, for I knew that a young girl would bring those same admirable qualities into marriage. These girls wound up in my mental black book of possibilities.

The rest of my life started that day I walked away from the wonderful lady who would be in charge.

If you think I was a little overboard, I beg to differ. I had determined I wanted the best marriage possible. So I did my homework. Did I want to spend my life waiting on a pitiful wife or dealing with weird emotional issues? No. I wanted a partner to share my vision and responsibilities. I wanted someone to HELP me do what I needed to do in life and ministry. So I checked out every possible girl, watching, waiting (not long), and considering. It was a tantalizing time in developing manhood, dreaming of my very own EVE.

When I was twenty years old, I finally settled on the most virtuous and attractive of all the girls I knew. She did have hair a little too short, but she looked mighty fine. She could play the piano and had a real nice singing voice. She was in big demand and stood out in any crowd. We had been brought up in the same church, I knew her family, and she knew mine. After observing her for some time and getting to know her in one-on-one conversations, I became convinced I couldn't live without her.

I decided to take the plunge. One evening after church, with the ring in my pocket, I took her home in the family station wagon. I was filled with wild anticipation. A man doesn't really feel like he has arrived until the day he finally finds his other half. God says he created them male and female, in his image. The longer I live, the clearer it is that a man is just not all there until he has his wife. My moment had arrived.

> *I learned that what I wanted for myself was not altogether what God wanted for me.*

I took Sweet-thing's tiny hand in mine and looked deep into her dark brown eyes. I smiled, knowing she was waiting and knowing what I was about to say. So knowing the answer, I asked her if she would be my wife, and with shining eyes she accepted my proposal. But the next day, as we contemplated our future together, she wanted my assurance that I would always be a Southern Baptist preacher. I was already ordained and licensed as a Southern Baptist preacher, and until that moment it had never occurred to me to be anything else. To be or not to be a Southern Baptist preacher was of no concern, but I was very much alarmed by her readiness to place frivolous conditions upon our future together. I was God's man, period, and would not limit him nor accept any limits upon my future.

An old preacher once told me that if you are seeking the Lord and walking in truth, yet a girl wants to change one thing about you before you marry, then you might as well plan on being her "whatever" all your life, because you surely will not be your own man. This wasn't exactly her trying to change me, but it was a forecast of things to come.

Several days transpired with very sober discussions; she tried to retract her demand. Other issues came up, and what took two years to develop, undeveloped in a few days. My Sweet-thing was not the one. I hoped things would turn around, but we grew in different directions. It took me a year or two to get over her. Sure, I felt like crud. I've got feelings just like the next guy. You haven't loved more than I, or been hurt more. Every guy thinks his heartbreak is the cruelest. It is difficult to think with your brains and not your emotions.

Many men drop the ball right here. They sense that something is not right. They wait for a better time to break it off with the girl. Maybe they even break up, but loneliness drives them back. Time passes and it gets harder and harder to cut the string, and then one day you wake up married and she is in control. Some things have to be done right the first time, and marriage is one.

I walked away a disappointed lover, but how much better than being a bound, dissatisfied husband? It was a very wise move, though I didn't feel wise at the time. No

No regrets. That is the key in life—no regrets.

regrets. That is the key in life—no regrets. Most men spend their life looking over their shoulder, wondering what might have been. You are young, just getting started in life. It is your time to make your own decisions and not let your life be ruined by your own action or inaction. I have been the captain of my life, and my wife has been my first mate. The rest of my life started that day I walked away from the wonderful lady who would be in charge.

If a girl attempts to direct your life, tell her to get a puppy, and then move on. And keep in mind that if she gets her feelings hurt because you don't do this thing or dress as she likes, then, buddy, you'd better run. Simple things can really get out of control once you are married.

So the lesson I learned was: You are not complete unless you have a woman, BUT it needs to be the right gal. I also learned that what I wanted for myself was not altogether what God wanted for me.

Young men need to be wise in realizing it takes wisdom to see things as they really are. At this time I know of several young ladies that, from all practical appearances, would be choice brides. The young, unsuspecting man would look upon these fair damsels and think they are more spiritual, pure, and well trained than any female they ever met. Maybe so, but the overall package is an illusion. Guys need to notice if a girl is moody, has general disrespect for men, or, most importantly, has a high opinion of herself as being the best catch, thinking any man would be lucky to have her. As an older man I know all this is a recipe for a very controlling, unhappy wife. Her long hair, modest clothing, high convictions, and sweet smile can cover a multitude of coming sorrow. There is more to choosing a bride than what you can write down on a what you want in a bride list.

Ask God for wisdom . . . right now as you are reading this.

On a side note, the list I had tucked in my head for the perfect bride flew the coop when I finally found my suitable other half. My little lady can't sing a lick, can't play the piano, and is cool only in a country girl way. But she is no one's second (but mine) and is ready for any challenge without whining or complaining. She is a real tiger when the door is shut, and that counts for a lot. As it turns out, in my life and ministry I never really needed a piano player or singer. What I needed was different, and that's what I got. More on that later.

P.S. Two years after the canceled proposal I was the pastor of an Independent Baptist church where I had a very successful ministry with hundreds saved and baptized every year. That is where I met my sweet, smart, and loyal little thing that I eventually married. Actually "sweet" is not a good adjective for her. She is too active and aggressive to be sweet all the time. I found I like extra lemon in my lemonade.

TIME TO CONSIDER:

The moral of this story is threefold.

1. Make it a habit to pray for WISDOM as if your life depends upon it—it does. Without wisdom I would not have seen the red flags when my Sweet-thing made her Southern Baptist demand.

2. Make it a habit to pray for COURAGE to do God's will regardless of how you feel, and never hesitate to walk away when there is doubt, regardless of bad timing or her tears. If a thing is of God, then plow forward. If you suspect it might not be God's perfect will, then consider it sin to continue the relationship. I could have let hormones and emotional attachment seal a relationship that I suspected was not God's will.

3. Pray, asking God to lead you to the woman who will be the perfect help meet for you. Don't create a list that God might deem unnecessary. Value what God values.

Eternal Questions:

"Since I was seeking God, and she seemed to be a good match, and my parents were for the relationship, why didn't God let me know sooner?

"Why was it all such a touch-and-go mystery?

"What would have happened if I had listened when she tried to retract her demands? Is there only one woman for me and do I have to find that perfect one?"

Remember Proverbs 3:5–6, **"Trust in the LORD with all thine heart; and lean not unto thine own understanding. In all thy ways acknowledge him, and he shall direct thy paths."** The key is to turn when he turns.

You were created to live
as part of a unit of two.

Chapter 6

WHAT IS A HELP MEET?

Before we launch into a list of things to look for in a help meet, we must review in more detail the meaning of the term help meet. I hear you saying, "Help meet? That sounds kind of archaic and religious. I don't know if that is what I am searching for or not. Give me a modern translation of help meet."

Adam was created to need a helper. Existing alone, he was incomplete and he knew it. Since the text says, **"there was not found an help meet for him"** it implies he felt his need and was searching for his counterpart. Thus the title of this book—*In Search of a Help Meet*. Herein lies the definition of help meet. Adam needed a helper that was meet for him—specially suited for him, appropriate to his needs.

Notice that it is two words, not one. Look at the words individually and then put them together. *Help* as in helper, and *meet* as in two things fitly joined together, as an upgrade meets the program for which it was designed. Adam was the program; Eve was the upgrade. The upgrade is not helpful without the program, and the program is incomplete without the upgrade. That is not a perfect analogy, so don't try to run with it.

You were created to live as part of a unit of two. God's human creation in his likeness is **"male and female."** Genesis 1:27 God named the two of them Adam. Genesis 5:2 Mr. Adam and Mrs. Adam. Until you acquire your bride, you are incomplete, bearing just half of

God's likeness. Before I married, I always felt incomplete, that life was in front of me, waiting to begin. In a social and emotional sense, marriage was the beginning of my humanity.

It is as if God drafted plans for a human and then tore the blueprint in half. Each half was fabricated separately, able to function independently, but with an innate need for the other—each with a sense of incompleteness until joined in a new kind of oneness. Like two different and distinct odors, each with its own unique characteristics, but when mingled they create an entirely new fragrance far more excellent than the originals. Adam could not reach his full potential until joined with his mate—like fingers and a thumb. As Adam's body was incapable of reproducing his species, his spirit was incapable of fully expressing his humanity. Eve made him whole. You need to find your Eve.

> *If you are not oriented to make her your best friend, then don't punish a girl by marrying her and then consigning her to a life of loneliness.*

Be warned, there is a general misunderstanding among both men and women as to the nature of a help meet. Eve was not created just to carry extra weight on the trail, or to speed up the process of gathering firewood, or to dry the figs Adam picked, as useful as those things may be. Two men could do physical labor together just as effectively. A wife is meant to be something much more than an assistant in the business of life. She is not God's wedding gift of a lifetime servant or an extra hand on the farm or in business. Eve was created to be the helper of Adam's soul, to complete his personality and emotional being.

What to Look for in a Help Meet

You need a help meet in more ways than just a sanctified lover. You will have to be married for some time before you discover how that little lady can meet those needs you don't yet know you have. So we are going to examine some of the qualities you should expect in your future mate.

Marry Your Best Friend

You may not be aware of it, but in time you will discover that you need your wife to be your best friend. Someone will be your best friend, and a wife is not happy unless she is that one special person with whom you

Without a best-friend relationship, sex is not an expression of love.

enjoy spending time. When your wife has a need, be assured, you have a need to fulfill it. If you care about her, you will care about the things she cares about. She cares very much to be your friend; it is her nature to feel so. It is also a good idea to keep in mind where your bread is buttered, your bed is made, and your creativity is birthed. A good man is rooted in God and a good woman. The bride spoke of her relationship to her beloved husband: **"This is my beloved, and this is my friend, O daughters of Jerusalem."** Song of Solomon 5:16 When your lover is not your friend, it makes her feel like a mistress being used—a "kept" woman.

Busy Girls Are Balanced

The young lady whom you will marry will already be deeply engaged in a life of her own. She will have close friends with whom she confides. There will be people who care about what she thinks who are willing to spend a great deal of time listening to her chatter about things that are important to

If she is not a good friend before marriage, she is not likely to become a friend afterward.

her. She will have one special friend with whom she shares her most personal self. She has not lived an isolated life, not been home alone all day. She has been a social creature, buzzing about here and there. When you marry her, you will remove her from all of her friends and family and place her in your circle. As such, you will now bear the responsibility to meet all her needs—her chief need being a best friend.

Your wife will need a best friend to listen to her sometimes-empty chatter and think she is wise and wonderful. When courting, a young man is content to spend hours just staring into those beautiful eyes as she talks about who-cares-what, but after a man's sexual drive is satisfied, he sometimes develops an attitude that says, "Can't you just be quiet until I need you again?" That attitude can produce a lot of hurt in a young bride, and it may become the seed that produces weeds that choke a marriage into crop failure.

Woman was created to be the helper of Adam's soul, to complete his personality and emotional being.

She will need a best friend whom she can trust with her fears and misgivings. You will be her best friend. If not, you will be a lousy husband. You cannot expect her to suddenly live in emotional isolation. Her life should change with you becoming the center of it. And if you are not oriented to make her your best friend, then don't punish a girl by marrying her and then consigning her to a life of loneliness.

I recently read the Facebook page of a 35-year-old girl about to marry for the first time. She posted this note: "To all my friends in the book club, and to all my friends at the exercise class, and all my friends at church, and those of you who have read my blogs, and to the girls and guys in my music class—bye-bye."

Knowing the girl, I could see her grinning while uttering her departing good-byes as she "put away childish things" to become the woman of her dreams, loving and serving the man in her life. She didn't feel she was giving up anything any more than a teenager feels the loss of parking his bike to drive his first car. She was "moving on up" and not looking back. That is the way it ought to be. She is not moving into a void unless you provide the void by treating her as a domestic servant who is supposed to sit at home all day waiting for you to come home so she can serve you dinner and sex.

A Friend in Deed

Some husbands so value their freedom that they are content to farm out their wives until needed. Wanting to avoid any emotional demands, they encourage their wives to seek a best friend in another young married woman or in a sister or mother. Under those circumstances the young couple never bond. One day the husband will be shocked to discover that she doesn't really need him and will choose the company of others (family or another girlfriend) over him. For a female, from the very beginning of marriage, friendship is love; being a helper is love. Without this relationship, sex is not an expression of love. A close friendship with her spouse is necessary in order for a female to find fulfillment in sex. When a husband doesn't make his wife his best friend she will become less responsive to his needs, and will come to not really care. Most young men fail to make or keep their wife as their best friend when it is easiest to do so— right after their marriage. Both, wife and husband, need to find a best friend in each other. It is the foundation of a good life and a great marriage.

I needed my best friend to be my bride.

Men assume that the sex drive that brings them back to moments of intimacy will also motivate the wife to forget all the negative feelings and just "make love," but men and women are not created the same. Females need tenderness and emotional goodwill to be sexually intimate. A man can separate the raw act of sex from love and fellowship, but most women cannot. You must tend to all her emotional needs if you expect her to tend to your physical needs. Don't make the mistake so many make of marrying a girl because she "turns you on." If she is not a good friend before marriage, she is not likely to become a friend afterward.

Personal

I was twenty-five years old, almost twenty-six, when I married Deb, my wife. I had known her well for four years, but not as a girlfriend. I became pastor of her home church when I was twenty-two years old. At the time, she was just seventeen and still in high school. I had my eye on several other girls closer to my age and considered several of them to be possibilities, but Deb did not get my attention as a prospective bride. She was just an immature kid who was not yet "cool."

The whole church was very active in evangelism, and I always had a station wagon full of kids, taking them here and there to pass out tracts or witness to sinners. When it came to sharing the gospel, Deb was the leader of the pack. So I came to depend upon her to organize the teenagers and plan events.

Like two odors that are sometimes smelled separately, when they are completely mingled they create a new fragrance far more excellent than the originals.

From time to time I brought along a girlfriend from college or some other church. So there were times when Deb was sitting in the front seat with us or maybe right behind us. I didn't know—had no idea—that Deb had already set her sights on me and was sure we would be married someday. Listen guys, that is a mistake you don't want to make. I heard about that for twenty years after we were married. She knew all my girlfriends by name. Some of them I forgot, but she didn't. Ten years later she would be telling me what was wrong with some girl I dated only once, and I couldn't even remember the girl she was talking about. **"[F]or love is strong as death; jealousy is cruel as the grave: the coals thereof are coals of fire, which hath a most vehement flame."** Song of Solomon 8:6 I know that's right.

As pastor, from time to time I found myself needing to visit in a home where a man was not present, so I always made sure I had someone with me to protect everyone's honor and reputation, especially mine. I never so much as stepped upon the porch of a home if I didn't know the man of the house was present. And I never walked through the door unless he was in sight or I could hear his voice inviting me in. So Deb came to be my cover, my assistant, my reputation guardian. When I was teaching Bible studies or preaching outside our church, I would take her along to counsel any girls that expressed a need. In short, we became best buddies, good friends. We shared the same interest and passion for winning people to Christ.

Still, I didn't see her as a potential spouse. She was just the big kid that I liked very much, and I even confided in her concerning my girlfriends. Wow! Was I dumb! Then one Sunday afternoon just after church I got struck a blow that I didn't see coming.

She Was MY Friend

Deb's parents had been ministering to service men and women long before I met them and became pastor of the church. Living about five miles from the Millington Naval Air Station where 40,000 guys were getting their schooling in preparation for deployment to Vietnam, every Sunday twenty or so guys came for a big dinner at Deb's house. Many of them had been converted to Christ, and some had grown to be mighty men of God. From time to time, one of the girls in the church would marry one of the guys. Soon she would be gone and we would see her no more.

On this particular Sunday, I walked in to a very busy house, everyone waiting for Mrs. Smith's famous pot roast, when suddenly in front of me bounced Deb and Randy—his name I remember. Randy had been stationed there for over a year and had become a vital assistant in the ministry, leading other guys to Christ. He was handsome and intelligent, greatly respected. He and I had worked together closely, even taking an extended kayak trip together down the Mississippi River. Deb was clinging to his arm as they stood in front of me and cheerfully announced that they were getting married.

Why not? She was now twenty; he was a fine man and would make her a great husband. I should have been glad for them, but something knotted up inside. I didn't recognize my unexpected reaction. It just couldn't be; she was MY friend. She was supposed to be there always. I felt the emptiness of her not being in my life. I had a girlfriend at the time, so why did I feel that way? It was the loss of a very dear friend I was feeling.

To be gloriously united to a woman is man's greatest fulfillment.

I stuttered and said something like, "Naaa, you're kidding." Several others gathered round to give their assent to the announcement. I think everyone saw that day what I had not even considered—I loved my best friend. I needed her. I couldn't live without her. Just as I felt like shaking them both and telling them that they were making a mistake, everybody began to laugh. It was all a joke on their pastor. I felt an overwhelming relief and quickly turned away, hoping my feelings were not flashing like red lights. I liked our relationship as best friends but had not thought of her as a bride. She still seemed too young and immature, but now I began to see her in a whole different light. For years before this, about once a month, an older woman in the church had told me, "You can't see the tree for the forest." She was right. Still, I waited several more months before admitting all that I felt that Sunday afternoon. I needed my best friend to be my bride. It was the wisest decision I ever made. The fact is I had to grow up and gain wisdom and understanding in order to see that she was indeed God's best for me.

Marriage Is God's Gift

To be gloriously united to a woman is man's greatest fulfillment. Until a man is married he is not finished. Until a man is happily married to a woman who thinks he is wonderful, he is simply not complete. Jesus so highly values marriage that he uses it as a pattern for his relationship to us, his church. We are the bride and he is the groom. There is an entire book in the Bible, The Song of Solomon, that discussing the intense union of a man and woman. It is there just so we would be advised as to how powerful a draw the male and female amalgamation truly is. I wrote a commentary on it called *Holy Sex*.

> *Jesus so highly values marriage that he uses it as a pattern for his relationship to us, his church.*

For you young men sitting on the threshold of this glorious time in your life, I salute you. It is all that Song of Solomon says, and more. You are like Adam struggling through the garden of your life knowing something is not finished but fearing an ugly result if you choose the wrong Eve and she ends up bringing you shame or unhappiness. There is so much ugliness in the world today, and marriage is just one of the things that is suffering as a result of the nation's turn away from God and holiness. Don't let fear steal the most precious gift God has for you in this life. Go for the gold, find a help meet; love her with all your heart. Here are some thoughts to guide you in your search.

TIME TO CONSIDER:

Search for this one:

A girl who has a heart bursting
with joy and gladness.

A girl who has a good relationship
with her dad.

A girl who is liked by her brothers.

A girl who is not lazy or lacking direction.

A girl who, according to the married folks, likes kids.

A girl who is joyful. I said that already, but it bears repeating.

Pass this one by:

A girl who is trying to change you. Drop her.

A girl who is sulky or moody. Run fast.

A girl who is judgmental. Let some other poor sucker
have her.

A girl who talks negatively about her dad. She will do the
same to you.

*Both—wife and husband—
need to find a best friend in
each other. It is the foundation
of a good life and a great
marriage.*

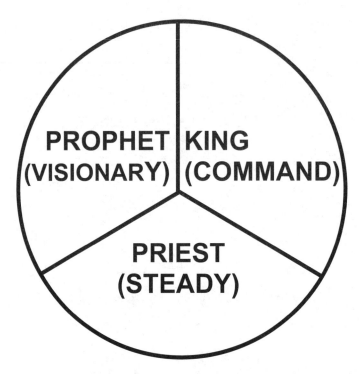

The Three Male Images

---

*And God said, let us
make man in our image,
after our likeness.*

Genesis 1:26

Chapter 7

KNOW YOUR IMAGE

Knowing your image type—those traits unique to your human nature—will dramatically clear up some confusing areas of your life. It also will help you understand what kind of gal will best suit you.

Created in His Image

At the beginning of the Bible God tells us that he created man in his own image: **"And God said, let us make man in our image, after our likeness."** Genesis 1:26 You are by nature in the image of God. You are in God's likeness. I know you have heard it said many times, but think about it for a moment. Ask yourself some questions: How am I like God? Do I look like him? Act like him? What does image mean?

An image is what looks back at you from the mirror. You have heard people say about some boy, "He is the spitting image of his dad." Now consider this: You are the spitting image of God. That demands some contemplation. It is difficult to wrap my mind around that concept even though it is clearly stated in God's Word.

Men come in all shapes and sizes, and vary in every aspect of personality, likes/dislikes, aptitudes, and drives; men are so very different from one another. Some males are very competitive, dominant, and commanding, sometimes to the point of excessively controlling. Other men are so focused on one issue they are weird, like a mad scientist or a dysfunctional geek. Others are so laid back and relaxed that you want to build a fire under them. So the image of

God finds many expressions.

Did you notice that verse in Genesis that said **"let us make man in our image"**? Who is the US and the OUR? Why does God use the plural when he speaks of himself? No error in the Scripture; it was clearly intended.

Strange as it may seem, answering these questions will help you understand who you are and what your calling is. Understanding your image and likeness will help you find a woman that suits your nature and your calling.

Profound Differences

The profound differences in the way men in God's image view and approach life help us understand why God said us. As a man ages, his peculiar nature becomes much more pronounced. Likewise, when a man marries, his personal image begins to become more apparent.

We will find our answers in the Bible. God set these differences into existence the day he created the first man. Genesis 1:26 says, **"And God said, Let us make man in our image, after our likeness."** You have taken note of the word us. Now notice the words *our image* and *our likeness*. God was making sure that no one could tamper with the passage and take out the *us* because the *our* would still be there. It is clear and simple: God is three

> *Who you are will determine what your marriage and family will be.*

persons in one. He is God the Father, King of the universe, Lord of lords. The kingly image of God takes command.

God is also Jesus, the Savior, Healer, the forgiving High Priest, the same yesterday and forever, steady and unchanging. The third expression of God is the Holy Spirit, who woos and convicts like the prophets of old. This part of God's image is visionary in nature. So we have three distinct images: King, Priest, and Prophet. God the Father is King. God the Son is the Priest. God the Holy Spirit is the Prophet. In combination, this threefold Godhead is the image of God that constituted the pattern for the creation of our human natures. Some men are more like the Father in their kingly command. Others are more like the Son in their priestly, steady natures. And some are like the Holy Spirit in his prophetic, visionary nature.

An image is what looks back at you from the mirror.

We are reluctant to dub men as King, Priest, or Prophet in nature, since we are indeed fallen creatures and seldom demonstrate anything noble in our natures. It seems more appropriate to call the King image Mr. Command man, for both the good and the bad, the Hitlers and the Churchills, are commanding in their natures. Likewise, there are few men in their fallen state that would fit the Prophet image, but those of that type, no matter how unrighteous they may be, are still Visionary in nature—whether for good or ill. So it is with those created in the Priestly image of Christ. The fallen, Priestly man remains more compassionate and sensitive in his nature, identifying with the hurts and ills of others. He is the Steady man among us. So we generally refer to the three types as Command (King), Visionary (Prophet), and Steady (Priest). That fits the good, the bad, and the ugly. One's nature for good has equal potential for evil. It is in

How do you determine which image you are most like?

knowing your nature with its strengths and weaknesses that you can best learn to relate to your wife in productive and not destructive ways.

How do you determine which image you are most like? Many young boys readily manifest their natural image, even from birth.

Mama gives it away when she says, "My son is so full of himself; he tells me what to do! How should I deal with him?" She just revealed that her son is a commander, created in the image of God the Father. He is in the King image—a Command man. Another mama will say of her son, "Well at least your son doesn't take your clocks apart trying to see why they make a ticking noise, or stick a pin in the electric socket." There is a Visionary at work. Later in life he will be espousing some great cause to set the world right.

> *Just as a man learns to read, he learns to reflect other images.*

Still another mama will smugly remark, "You ladies need to read the book *To Train Up a Child* by Michael Pearl. I read it, and my little Johnny never bosses me or takes things apart." She doesn't know it has little to do with her training but much to do with his God-given nature as a Steady, Priestly little man waiting for a chance to express his compassion and mercy when he grows up.

What these moms don't know is that their little men are already showing their stuff. The bossy fellow is just exercising his image of God the Father and will naturally always take Command. The curious little guy is created in the image of the Holy Spirit, and he will be a Visionary, wanting to see and know truth. The boy who is obedient and kind reflects the image of Jesus, and he will be a Steady fellow and most likely a follower rather than a leader. Each boy has weaknesses and strengths that reflect his image. As the boy matures, he will learn to curb his natural drives in order to keep out of trouble or keep from being bullied, or from being labeled a bully.

Many of you are casting around in your mind, wondering if you missed your image. You haven't. Just as a man learns to read, he learns to manifest other images. For instance, a Visionary boy with a kind, Steady dad will learn balance from his dad if they have a good relationship. If he spends some time with his commanding granddad, he will pick up on leadership qualities. He will be so balanced that it will be hard to put a tag on him. A gentle, laidback son will develop a little leadership if he has spent a lot of time with his commanding dad. A young man might like to lead but hesitate to step up because his dad, whom he greatly admires, is a quiet, Steady man; the young boy naturally emulates his dad. Boys who grow up with good, wholesome relationships with their dads, granddads, and other men will be more balanced, unless, of course, all the men around them are Visionaries.

In studying people for years, it is obvious that most people are predominantly one type but a little of one or the other. You may see a Command man that is a little bit Visionary, so he takes charge but also has a vision of changing things. Therein is the making of the most dominant personalities in history. You may also see a Command man that has a little Steady (Priestly) in him. He will take the lead in directing men in works of compassion. The first mix will be general in war and the second will be the Surgeon General.

Why do types or images matter anyway?

Why do types or images matter anyway? None of us is totally balanced. When you have an idea of your image, it is a relief to see you are just as God created you to be. It is also a wake-up call, because you will know your weakness as well as your strengths, enabling you to build on your strength and be cautious and attentive to your weaknesses. When a Steady man knows his image, he will understand why he likes the Go-to girls when Mr. Command thinks they are just bossy females.

As you read this, you will discover your image and you will note what kind of girl you gravitate toward. You will then be able to choose a wife more wisely, having this information. If you still can't figure out your image, ask a few girls; they will enjoy picking you apart. Females, as a rule, are like that. Now, on to a study of the three images in which we are created.

I named the types of men after God's three images:

1. Prophet/Visionary
2. Priest/Steady
3. King/Command

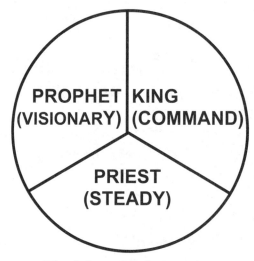

The Three Male Images

What About the Girlies?

Adam was formed from the dust of the earth. God actually breathed the breath of life into him, but not Eve. Adam had the whole human race in his loins, male and female. But he needed the other half of the race to procreate. Eve came from Adam's side, one of his ribs to be exact. She was the first clone—of a sort. She was, as Adam so wisely stated,

"...now bone of my bones, and flesh of my flesh: she shall be called Woman, because she was taken out of Man." Genesis 2:23

Eve derives her image of God through the image of the man from which she was taken.

Eve is in the image of God once removed—but a fact essential to note. Women are a softer, gentler version of God's image; the two, male and female coming together, become the complete image of God. By being softer (less rigidly fixed) it allows the woman to mesh with the man, and he to cherish her rather than compete with her. It is her role to be the helper. So yes, females come in the Prophet, Priest, and King images, only a more moldable version, able to adapt to what thier husbands will need. We call the female images: **Dreamers** (Visionary/Prophet), **Servants** (Steady/Priestly), and **Go-to** girls (Command/King).

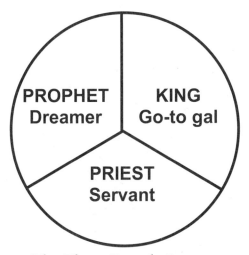

The Three Female Images

Although a godly woman will be moldable, there is less conflict and adjustment when a man marries a woman of a different image type. A Command/King husband that marries a strong Go-to/King gal will most likely experience some cataclysmic clashes. If a Steady/Priestly man marries a gentle, kind Servant/Priestly girl, they will lack the fortitude to raise their Command/King sons or daughters. When two Visionary/Prophets (Dreamer) marry, there will be no one with their feet on the ground to keep the dynamic duo stable. Although, sometimes two Visionaries can make an extraordinary couple, pounding like a two-piston engine, accomplishing great things together. But two Visionaries may end up in a ring, fighting for their ideas to be paramount. Later in this section I'll give you some examples of the issues, both good and bad, that arise from two people of the same image marrying each other.

Are you asking, "So how do I know what my sweetie is—Dreamer, Servant, or Go-to girl?" Things aren't as complicated as they sound. A Command/King guy almost never likes Go-to/Kingly type girls. He will be drawn to gentle-hearted Servant girls. Steady/Priestly men think Go-to girls are cute with their forceful, gotta-do list. Visionary men generally are attracted to stable girls instead of wild-dressing Dreamers. So it is with all the types. Dreamer girls like stable Steady men or strong, dependable Command men to take care of them. People are naturally drawn to what completes them. So even if you have no knowledge of the concept of image types, if you choose your own bride, you will like the kind of girl with whom you are most comfortable—an opposing image type. Troubles arise when you choose a girl for her sexuality before you get to know her as a person.

There is also the chance of getting poorly matched when you allow someone else to choose for you. If your father is a Command man, he is going to like a girl that is steady and faithful—a bit dull. But if you are a Steady fellow, you will like the Go-to gal because you find her drive to be just what you need, while Dad thinks the one you like is bossy. Obviously, Mother and Father are going to choose the types that please them, which may be the opposite of what will please you.

Are you asking, "So how do I know what my sweetie is—Dreamer, Servant or Go-to?"

*The knowledge of how to
handle your type will help
you make wise choices in
directing your life.*

TIME TO CONSIDER:

You are what you eat, think, and do. How you spend your days, hours, and minutes is who you are. What you fill your mind with is who you are. Whether you are a fat slob or a fit man of God depends on what you eat and what you do. Who you are will determine what your marriage and family will be.

Diagram this passage as if you will do a public reading of it.

Ecclesiastes 3:1-15

To every thing there is a season, and a time to every purpose under the heaven: A time to be born, and a time to die; a time to plant, and a time to pluck up that which is planted;

A time to kill, and a time to heal; a time to break down, and a time to build up; A time to weep, and a time to laugh; a time to mourn, and a time to dance;

A time to cast away stones, and a time to gather stones together; a time to embrace, and a time to refrain from embracing;

A time to get, and a time to lose; a time to keep, and a time to cast away; A time to rend, and a time to sew; a time to keep silence, and a time to speak;

A time to love, and a time to hate; a time of war, and a time of peace.

What profit hath he that worketh in that wherein he laboureth? I have seen the travail, which God hath given to the sons of men to be exercised in it.

He hath made every thing beautiful in his time: also he hath set the world in their heart, so that no man can find out the work that God maketh from the beginning to the end.

I know that there is no good in them, but for a man to rejoice, and to do good in his life. And also that every man should eat and drink, and enjoy the good of all his labour, it is the gift of God.

I know that, whatsoever God doeth, it shall be for ever: nothing can be put to it, nor any thing taken from it: and God doeth it, that men should fear before him.

That which hath been is now; and that which is to be hath already been; and God requireth that which is past.

It is not easy to be a good man,
a loving husband, and a faithful
father, so pray for wisdom.

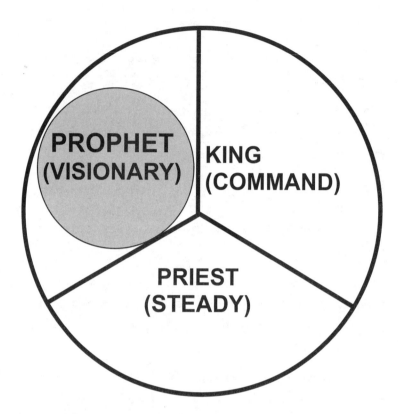

The Three Male Images

The Prophet or Visionary is the man who is "the voice of one crying in the wilderness."

Chapter 8

PROPHET/VISIONARY

God is a Prophet, as seen in his person the Holy Spirit. Some
of you men were created in this image. Are you a shaker, changer,
and dreamer? Everybody is disturbed by the direction our country
is taking, but the Visionary will become engaged trying to persuade
people and to change things, while the Steady man just gripes. Have
your mom and dad challenged you to use your time and energy on
other things rather than being focused on contentious issues?

The Prophet or Visionary is the man who is "the voice of one
crying in the wilderness," striving to change the way things are done,
or trying to change the way humanity is behaving or thinking. Often
the folks you think should be doing things differently are the ones
who love you best. You judge them. But all they see is the beam in
your eye.

Often a Prophet will come up with a new doctrine that he
knows is more important than any other issue, and he is amazed and
irritated that no one is listening to his warning. Prophet/Visionary
men are the preachers, political activists, organizers, and instigators of
any front-line social issue. They love confrontation and hate the status
quo. Life could be peaceful to the point of dull without Visionaries
(guys) and Dreamers (girls). Most Visionaries are consumed with the
need to communicate with words, music, writing, art, or actions.
Think of the focused musicians you know— most likely they are
Prophets/Visionaries. The Visionary always has a cause, and his

concern is unquestionably the most important, at least he thinks so. His focus can make him a bully.

If you are 100% this type, then you can rest assured that you are NOT dull. You will love with passion; you can be loyal to a fault and cry unashamedly. You are very opinionated. If you are open to advice and treat your wife and children with respect, they will think you are the smartest man on earth.

Two Good Sources of Balance

Most of your problems, as with all types, will result from your lack of balance. Balance in a man comes from two sources. It can first be found in good male examples and relationships when growing up. Those are the balancing years. If a boy misses adapting his propensities when young, he must learn to humble himself and admit that he might not see the whole picture. He should recognize his need to listen and learn from wise counsel. Second, if a man is willing to listen and learn from his wise wife, she can be a huge help to him. A Visionary will do better if he marries a woman with a little queenliness (Go-to) in her and a lot of the Servant. She needs to be willing to serve and please you but have the fortitude to give you what-for when you are totally off balance.

Don't go wife hunting until you have gone job hunting and are either gainfully employed or have a moneymaking business that will provide for her.

How do you recognize the Dreamer/Go-to mixture in a girl? It is easy to spot a Dreamer by the uncommon way she dresses. It is easy to spot a Priestly/Servant girl by the way she loves to please and serve folks. The Command/Go-to girl takes charge when opportunity arises. Look for a girl who shows strength but is taught to honor and serve. Look at her mom. Most girls pick up critical attitudes from their mothers, unless they have been taught God's Word concerning womanhood. Watch for that red flag. Prophet/ Visionaries do not do well under criticism (no one does) but Prophets really suffer. Yet most Prophet/Visionary men bring criticism on themselves with their weird notions—another reason they need a wife that is not part of that parade.

If you think you might be a Visionary type, then you need to look for a lady who has her feet firmly established on planet earth so you can depend on her to bring you back to reality when you get weird in pursuit of your vision. You need a plain-thinking woman, because your lack of balance will affect many relationships in your life. If you have a lady who can see both sides, and you give her the freedom to tell you what she really thinks, it will help you maintain and develop balance. After all, when you always think your way is the only way, it is bound to cause problems.

I Deserve It

The lack of balance could make you feel as if someone owes you something when they don't. It will cause you to focus on one or two odd ideas and, in the process, upset the entire family. Maybe you know a man who has a problem with balance in this area. He might harp on peripheral issues like Christmas being a pagan holiday. Hey, I agree, but is it worth a big fight? Or maybe a man will drive his wife into an early grave, standing firm on birth control. Put the man in her situation and, if he is honest, he would rethink his doctrine. Some Prophet-type men get into a fight with the Social Security system. This is SO NOT eternal; it's a losing battle.

The issues Visionaries focus on may be serious and worthy of one's attention but not obsession. In varying degrees these men can have tunnel vision, tenaciously focusing on single issues. In the long run, many unbalanced Visionaries cause their families to suffer needlessly. If this is you, begin to pray for wisdom, and then ask two or three wise, Steady men to advise you. Make a written promise to yourself to listen even when it seems they are dragging their feet. You need to seek balance. It is not easy to be a good man, a loving husband, and a faithful father, so pray for wisdom. The knowledge of how to handle your type will help you make wise life choices.

Visionary men are often either very rich or very poor. Usually they don't make the best employees but do better working for themselves. Of course, some Visionaries find a niche at a plant where they can work long hours, creating, expanding, and solving problems.

Don't expect your new bride to swoon with wonder at your wild ideas.

When that happens, they are extremely valuable employees. The assembly line is not for Visionaries. A "same-old" routine drives them up the wall. But be assured, when he comes down he will have modified the smoke detector.

A Visionary born 150 years ago might have been a pioneer, explorer, or inventor. I imagine that mountain men and gold prospectors were Visionaries also. They are not dull. A storekeeper making a modest weekly income would not be a Visionary, and that type is never the hero in the movies. The task of storekeeping would be too tame for the wild streak that runs in the veins of most Visionaries, unless, of course, the Visionary had found balance and was trying to start a chain that would make him rich. Then he could enjoy speculating on a store, but he would hire a Steady man to run it for him.

Adam Was NO Sluggard

God didn't create Adam to sit around under the fruit trees, making love and eating peaches and avocados. He was a legal immigrant enlisted to work in a garden. Genesis 2:7 God appointed Adam, not Eve, to **"till the ground from whence he was** taken." ^{Genesis 3:23} **"And the LORD God took the man, and put him into the garden of Eden to dress it and to keep it."** ^{Genesis 2:15} **"In the sweat of thy face shalt thou eat bread, till thou return unto the ground; for out of it wast thou taken: for dust thou art, and unto dust shalt thou return."** ^{Genesis 3:19}

So Adam, not Eve, was the one given responsibility to do the labor that provided for the family. It was *his* face that would sweat, and *he* who should till the ground.

Paul confirms the duty of man: **"For even when we were with you, this we commanded you, that if any would not work, neither should he eat. For we hear that there are some which walk among you disorderly, working not at all, but are busybodies."** 2 Thessalonians 3:10-11

"But if any provide not for his own, and specially for those of his own house, he hath denied the faith, and is worse than an infidel." 1 Timothy 5:8

That pretty wells says it. God created men to work and earn their living by the sweat of their faces, and if a man doesn't work, no one should feed him. We should call him an infidel and let him starve. Pretty serious, wouldn't you say? I think there is a good case here for saying that God expects you to be active making your way in life, not depending on your parents or hers, and not living off of the government dole.

A man can't live without love, but neither can he live on it. Love will not put food on the table or pay for the insurance or put new tires on the automobile.

Therefore, before you get engaged to a girl, you should be fully engaged in making your own way in life. If you cannot support yourself and maintain a house and automobile and pay all the bills and have some left over to put away for your honeymoon, you should not consider marriage.

Can't Find a Job?

Can't find a job? That's too bad, because as the man in the family, it is your responsibility to provide for your own house. Don't let this become a major flaw in your life. Don't go wife hunting until you have gone job hunting and are either gainfully employed or have a moneymaking business that will provide for her.

The demands of marriage are a gift from God to force us into assuming responsibility. Married life relentlessly places demands upon the man to perform and provide. You are ready to copulate, but are you ready to operate the family business? It is your show, sink or swim, cheap rental or four acres in the suburbs; it's all in your hands. Where do you buy used washing machines? Who repairs refrigerators? How do you fix the plumbing or get a worn-out lawn mower started? Should you try to fill out your own income taxes or try to save up $150 to pay someone to do it? Can you conduct banking and balance your budget? Where can you cut back, or should you try to work a second job? The wife is sick; should you take her to the doctor or wait it out? Welcome to responsibility. Are you up to it?

Don't Panic

No, wait! Don't run away. Every first marriage started with two inexperienced people. It is your youthful energy and low expectation that will take the edge off the seemingly daunting things you will face. As I look back on the first two years of my marriage, I wonder how my wife tolerated it. Come to think of it, sometimes she didn't. But we were in love and had the energy to keep trying until we got the hang of it. It was worth every minute—the good and the bad. I do not want to discourage you from getting married, but I do want to encourage you to do more to get yourself ready for the ironman marathon of matrimony.

Many godly women are suffering needlessly at the hands of a disobedient man who will not work. If you are a young man reading this and know of a Visionary who has not kept a job or supported himself, yet he is planning to marry, PLEASE warn the girl's family. Give them this book and have it clearly marked. Tell them this is why you are speaking out. He can still be your friend once he gets over being mad. Just do the right thing.

Leaving and Cleaving

When you get married you will be subject to the very first commandment given by the first prophet upon the earth. Adam said: **"Therefore shall a man leave his father and his mother, and shall cleave unto his wife: and they shall be one flesh."** Genesis 2:24

This is a most significant prophecy and commandment, seeing how Adam did not have a father and mother to leave. He foresaw the future structure of society and knew that it would require something painful for him as a father; his sons would leave him both physically and jurisdictionally to commence their own independent families,

Many marriage problems would be solved if the simple rule of leaving and cleaving were obeyed.

and his daughters would leave him and become one flesh with their husbands. Children are born to be given away in marriage. They give back with their grandchildren.

"And Jesus answering said unto them, The children of this world marry, and are given in marriage:" Luke 20:34

Some parents, usually mamas, become emotionally dependent upon their children and find it very difficult to give them away in marriage. The happier and more contented an older couple is in marriage, the easier it is for them to allow their children to leave home and cleave to their spouses. When a marriage is not very fulfilling, parents can transfer all their affection to their children and suffer emotionally when the children pull away in marriage. Thus the sins of the parents can cause grief to the new couple. Clinging and cleaving are two sides of a coin. Don't allow your mama to maintain a tight relationship with you once you are married. Cozy talks with mama can be just as damaging as an adulterous affair with the secretary; they are stealing that which belongs to your bride.

Mamas Cleaving with Mamas

These clinging mamas can do damage during courtship as well. It can be especially difficult if both the mama of the prospective groom and the bride are clingy. If the two mamas get together to bond then you have a recipe for a sure break in the young couple's relationship. The young man and woman come together to create an entirely new family—not to add to one or the other of the existing families. Do you sense trouble in paradise? Remember: your in-laws will be YOUR in-laws; they will be NO kin to your father and mother, thus there is no reason for the two older couples to bond. They can become happily acquainted briefly, but there are plenty of reasons for the two older couples NOT to CLEAVE to each other; the case has been proven through a thousand letters to our ministry. Over the twenty or so years that we have been working with people concerning marriage, THE most damaging issue in the new marriage is not adultery or drugs or porn, it is the son (and sometimes the daughter) maintaining a bond with Mama. Just talking, just sharing your fears and joys, and just letting mama know how needful she is to you is not leaving and not cleaving. *Cleave* is the word God used. So cleave—cut the tender relationship off with a big cleaver.

Leave and Cleave

Jesus reaffirmed Adam's prophecy/commandment found in Genesis 2:24.

And said, For this cause shall a man leave father and mother, and shall cleave to his wife: and they twain shall

be one flesh? Wherefore they are no more twain, but one flesh. What therefore God hath joined together, let not man put asunder.
Matthew 19:5-6

Paul also quotes the "leave and cleave" passage in Ephesians 5:31. This word *cleave* is most powerful. All you need do is look up the word in a concordance and read every time it is used in the Authorized Version—46 times in all. Only the Authorized Version preserves the original Hebrew meaning by translating *dabaq* as cleave. We don't need original language helps to come to that conclusion. Of course if you use the NIV you won't find the word cleave used even once, and you are left with no cross-references. Ignorance begets ignorance. Thank God for an accurate, up-to-date translation in the Authorized Version.

The NIV translates *dabaq* as cling, plague, hold fast, ally, stuck to, defiled, stick, opened up, reduced to, joined, bound, remain united, split, remain true. The lack of serious scholarship is appalling but typical of any commercial version.

DON'Ts for the Prophet/Visionary

1. Don't marry until you can support your own family.

2. Don't consider marrying until you are ready to leave your family and stand on your own two feet.

3. Don't even think of putting your new bride into a situation where she has to be under your mother's or father's authority or roof. When you marry, honor God by honoring the counsel he set in place. He said, **"Therefore shall a man leave his father and his mother, and shall cleave unto his wife: and they shall be one flesh."** Genesis 2:24 The word *leave* means leave, so don't bother using the Greek to try to reinvent the meaning.

Another important consideration: Don't marry a girl whose parents insist that she stay close to them. If her parents push the issue, make your intentions perfectly clear; they are giving their daughter to you in holy matrimony, which means she is yours and you will take her wherever God leads you. Have a clear and very positive affirmation from your sweetie that she totally agrees with you. Pray with her on the matter so that she understands she is making a promise before God to leave her father and mother, and so are you. Most girls are anxious to leave; usually it is the young man hanging on to Mommy's apron strings and Daddy's rent-free guesthouse.

Our ministry receives thousands of letters seeking help for hurting marriages, so we know what is causing lasting problems. As I said, this issue is at the top of the list. Many problems in marriage could instantly be solved if both the man and his new bride obeyed this simple rule of leaving and cleaving.

Mr. High and Low

Now that I have beaten you up, it is time for some encouragement. You will need a lot of encouragement as you mature, because you will most likely have some highs and lows that neither Mr. Steady/Priest nor Mr. Command/King will ever experience.

When you, Mr. Visionary, choose a bride, keep this in mind: Your honey will need to have an upbeat personality; no moody or melancholy gal will suit you. Temperamental females might be interesting and challenging, but you need a girl who is focused on the here-and-now. Forget the ones with puckered lips, even if those lips are adorable.

Temperamental females might be interesting and challenging, but you need a girl who is focused on the here-and-now.

If you are a Visionary, your inborn creativity will propel you to the top if you handle it correctly. You will see possibilities that other men just don't see. You might be an inventor or have a real gift for music or art. You may have the ability to see ways of making a factory run more efficiently, or you may be capable of designing a vehicle that travels to Mars. When you marry, you will love talking to your wife about all the things you envision that others just seem to totally miss. For that reason, she will put up with a great deal of nonsense from you. Women love men to talk to them. Most people miss the finer details of the thing that enthralls you; they simply don't have your focus. Keep in mind that you will always see as if looking through a tunnel. Like Pasteur, who discovered that rabies was caused by a virus, you will know there is a germ that is killing people because it just makes sense to you that something unseen is there. This type of understanding will seem simple to you, but it will be foreign to the average guy. God in his mercy gave some men this type of vision so the world would not grow stagnant; he knew we needed adventuresome men to scout out new lands, find a cure, climb the highest mountain, and call others to repentance.

Here's a clue in marriage: Don't expect your new bride to swoon with wonder at your wild ideas. She will not see the need to climb, investigate, or leave her cozy home for places unknown. Only your love, steadfast commitment, and wise decisions will give her enough confidence to believe you will take care of her and her little ones regardless of where you lead her. You will need to earn her trust. It will take time to make that happen, especially if she was raised by a Mr. Steady dad who worked 8 to 5 every day and never came up with a wild idea in his whole life. Let her be your project the first year, and after that you will have one person in the world who thinks you are brilliant, but still have the common sense to know that some of your wilder ideas are impractical.

Here's the Thing

Often the difference between a productive Visionary and a destructive one is a good, supportive, stable woman. But don't blame the little lady when you mess up your life, because she will be what you make her. If she is fearful, you have given her reason; if she is angry, most likely you have stirred up wrath. If she is bitter, ask yourself what you are doing that causes it. You will be the head of the household. Wisely choose a woman who will follow the leader, and then lead her to paths of love and peace.

In my book *Created to NEED a Help Meet*, I wrote this:

> "A radical Visionary can be saved from dead ends and useless eruptions by his wise help meet's simple words of caution—that is, if he hasn't converted her to his radical worldview. Visionaries are prone to see the world in black and white and can become critical of everyone around them. Some wives are influenced by their negative attitude and lose the ability to see clearly. He cultivates her into an amen corner for his attitude and actions when what he really needs is a smoke detector that sounds an alarm when his direction is likely to start a conflagration that will burn the entire family. If a man gripes about the pastor, his boss, politics, the church, the Illuminati, or the Bilderbergers long enough, he may encourage his wife to join him in his pessimism. Instead of controlling his fire, she fans it. An immature Visionary that believes in his own infallibility likes to smother his doubts with the blind affirmation of his wife. He wants his help meet to do all the meeting; he already knows what he must do, come hell or high water."

Most young guys reading this will have a hard time relating because, as of yet, you have not developed all-consuming ideas about politics, religion, or anything of import. That's because right now your main concern is fulfilling your male passions. But if you are the Visionary type, once you marry and have that problem off your mind, you will develop visions of grandeur that cloud your thinking and steal your peace. When you do get married, come back and read this book so you will be reminded of how to relate to your chosen lady.

In *Created to NEED a Help Meet* I listed the Five Ls for Mr. Visionary: Listen, Love, Laugh, Labor, and Leave. You would do well to read them (page 87) and make a copy of this in-a-nutshell list for Prophets. Stick the list on your fridge or in your Bible to help you remember when you marry how your strengths and weaknesses might affect your coming marriage.

The Wild Training of Visionary Preachers

I know of a Bible school where the founder and president of the school is an extreme Visionary, and nearly all the young men enrolled are Visionaries or constrained by example to become as much like them as possible. The men are not taught to control their image but rather to augment it without apology or restraint. Anything different from a 100% Visionary street preacher is a wimp. Thus when the men finish school, most all of them have trouble getting along with folks. They are full of rebuke and bombast. They have a divorce rate higher than average and a host of other issues that could easily be avoided with a little humility and appreciation for the other two types of men. Knowing several of them, I can say with authority that they generally lack respect for females. What is your life if you dishonor God in the one relationship on earth that is to mirror Christ and the church? Remember, your image type is never an excuse for imbalance. Regardless of your natural image, you are responsible to be a well-rounded man.

Time to Consider:

WORDS

Look up these key words where they appear in Scripture and learn from them.

Proverbs 13:2 "A man shall eat **good** by the fruit of his mouth: but the soul of the transgressors shall eat violence."

Proverbs 13:4 "The soul of the sluggard desireth, and hath nothing: but the soul of the **diligent** shall be made fat."

Proverbs 13:8 "The **ransom** of a man's life are his riches: but the poor heareth not rebuke."

Proverb 13:16 "Every **prudent** man dealeth with **knowledge**: but a fool layeth open his folly."

Proverb 13:18 "Poverty and shame shall be to him that refuseth instruction: but he that **regardeth reproof** shall be honoured."

Proverbs 13:20 "He that **walketh with wise men** shall be wise: but a companion of fools shall be destroyed."

Proverbs 13:22 "A **good man** leaveth an **inheritance** to his children's children: and the wealth of the sinner is laid up for the just."

Advice from the Girls . . .

A Silly Boy

"I know this guy who is tall and handsome, highly intelligent, and works hard supporting himself, but girls don't give him the time of day and he doesn't know why. His problem is his public acknowledgement of his first love. Most girls who are interested in a guy will research him on the social media. Girls share everything, so they pass the info along. Mr. Loveless spends a great deal of time raving about the latest comic book hero or some new graphic comic book or movie. He lives in a world of superheroes. It's his business to like whatever he chooses, but no girl wants to be tied to a man so shallow and empty. None of the girls give him the time of day. One girl who momentarily considered him, said, 'After I read his remarks, I thought, I can do better than this. Who needs tall and handsome? I want a man, not a silly boy.'"

More Advice from the Girls . . .

The Stalker

"There is this hot-looking guy that came to our church youth social. He is nice looking, not sissy or anything like that, but he just suddenly started staring at one of the really good-looking girls—I mean staring. She was embarrassed and even unnerved, like he was a stalker right there at church. A couple hours later when the meeting ended, her boyfriend came to pick her up and Mr. Stare shifted his gaze around at the other girls as if casting the net elsewhere, and guess what? I was his new focus. Duuuuh. It was obvious he didn't care about anyone but his own needs, just the best-looking chick he could snag. Even though I know an older person that says he is an okay guy, the stalker gave all us girls the creeps. Girls like to feel that the guy values them as a special girl, and if he can't have the one he wants, then he just is not interested, not because they are the prettiest either. Mr. Stare made me feel he was just after a babe and if I didn't bite the bait, well, there are plenty of fish in the sea. I know, I know. He is probably a weird Visionary-type artist or something, so we should just get over it, right? Wrong! I'll take a normal Steady/Priest who is scared to talk to me, but not a guy that stalks."

And a Little More . . .

Guys Ask: If I want to check out a girl going to a different church, how would I go about it?

Girls Answer: First get to know the leaders, which might mean coming to several meetings. The girls will ask their brothers about you. If the guys think you are a sober-minded, godly fellow with wholesome interests, they will tell their sisters, and the girls will talk about you and then seek to make an occasion for you to speak to them. Never stare at a girl; a quick glance catching her eye is very intriguing. You will learn from the guys which girl is available. Pay careful attention to what that girl does in her job or ministry. From the information you gather, decide which girl you want to get to know. When you have the opportunity, single her out for conversation, showing interest in her job or whatever she likes. Doesn't take a rocket scientist, but it does take a man who has interest in another human being and not just his own needs.

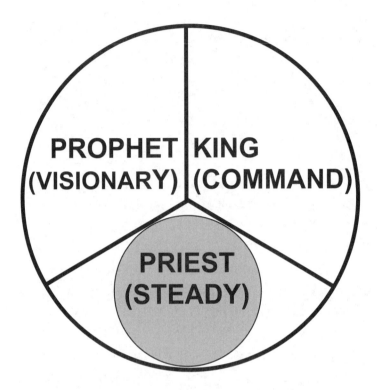

The Three Male Images

God the Son is as steady
as an eternal rock,
caring, providing, and
faithful in his ministry
as priest.

Chapter 9

PRIEST/MR. STEADY

Many of you breathed a sigh of relief as you read the last chapter because you knew you were not that type. You would NEVER walk into a church social and stare a girl down. You would never get on Facebook or any other social network and brag about something like a comic book. That would embarrass you to no end. You are just too clear-headed and plain thinking to fit most of the descriptions in the previous chapter. If so, then you may be a Priest/Steady type.

God the Son is as steady as an eternal rock, caring, providing, and faithful in his ministry as priest. He created many men in his priestly image. This type of man is the backbone of society, the middle ground that keeps the world moving on a steady course. You can depend on a Steady man. He is not given to wild anger, he doesn't demand others

> *Steady/Priestly men are the backbone of society.*

to follow him; he listens to all arguments and is slow to judge… as well as SLOW to make decisions. He is not given to extremes. Down South we call these men "good ol' boys" or "Bubba" (being interpreted: Good Brother) because they are.

If you are a Mr. Steady, you are not as likely to start your own business unless it slowly evolves from some steady occupation that you can do well. A solid, regular job with a weekly paycheck is what you prefer.

You know that you are not the most exciting man alive. In the evenings after work you like to hang out with your friends and shoot some basketball, play a few video games, or just watch a movie. If your church leaders organize and push, you would go along and pass out tracts, but you would not plan the event. Standing on the street corner yelling "Repent!" is not your style.

And on a more personal level, getting to know girls is a mystery to you. You do a lot of thinking, but not much comes of it. When you have an opportunity to talk to a girl, you usually find it uncomfortable and can't think of what to say. Take heart, my friend; she will find you. In your shyness you will attract aggressive girls, bossy girls—what my wife calls Go-to girls. You will like their style because their high-handedness amuses you. It takes different strokes for different folks, and Mr. Steady likes to be stroked by an aggressive gal. It leaves him free to be on the more comfortable receiving end of things. He doesn't have to force himself to act. She acts for him and upon him.

As a single man, you need to know that if a girl is sitting on her butt at home doing nothing to advance herself, then she is not your Proverbs 31 gal.

This makes some of you laid-back guys sitting ducks when it comes to the marriage hunt. You need to make some decisions now before the GIRLS pick YOU. You are not good at saying no to anyone for anything.

I am not going to tell you how imbalanced you are, because you're not. You can see your best friend's weirdness (Prophet/Visionary) and still think he is a fine, interesting guy. You enjoy helping your other friend with some of his projects (King/Command) even though he bosses you around. You enjoy seeing things happen, and because he is your friend, you know he will call on you whenever he has something big going on. You are a good, all-around buddy whom everyone likes.

You're not innately lazy, but neither are you motivated to push against resistance. You are not going to invest your last dime on a venture that might or might not make money.

You think you might be just a little boring. You are. Your future wife will think you are too, and it will drive her crazy. This will be your greatest challenge in marriage. So what does a man do if he bores his honey? And how can a young man plan his life to keep from boring his new bride? Of all the advice in this book, this answer will prove the most helpful if you make use of it: value her.

Value Her

This advice is key for all three images, but it is paramount for Mr. Steady. The Visionary will be the best at valuing his wife, although he may tend to misuse her. The Command man will lose big if he is too stiff and authoritarian to value his lady. A Steady man will keep his wife sickly, miserable, and bored if he neglects to value her. I wish I could make all you guys avoid the pitfalls of missing this one rule—value your wife.

So What Does Valuing a Female Mean?

Just this morning, I was listening to a friend share his recent Bible study on repentance. He was very excited about the things he was discovering and had produced a four-page study that he could share with others. He has had some conflict in his marriage because his wife felt she was not valued. In sharing with me how he had come to some of his conclusions, he mentioned that he had asked his wife to listen to his arguments and tell him if they were weak or strong. He said that for over an hour they had brainstormed together as she made some very astute observations that he incorporated into his written study. He felt that she had greatly facilitated the quality of his final draft. He said, "Wow! Did we have fun doing this thing together!"

Now I have spent several hours talking to him, trying to get him to see the need to value his wife in acts, not just words, and he had always missed the point. This was a breakthrough! I responded to his delight about their shared experience by saying, "That was foreplay."

His face screwed around in wonder like I had just come down with some weird disease, and he said, "Foreplay? Brother Mike, we were studying the Bible."

> *Being valued is just that—being a necessary partner in all aspects of life.*

I told him, "Valuing her and foreplay are equal to a woman. You finally valued your woman. It is what women love the most. You complimented her. You treasured her. But most of all, you valued her. You exalted her. You cherished her. You lifted her from dirty dishes and diapers to equal heir of the grace of God. You, my friend, allowed her to be your help meet. She helped you. She met your needs on an intellectual and spiritual level, a place that you have previously shut her out. So if you had reached over to kiss her, she would have been hot and ready—no holds barred." He is pretty thick-headed, so I seized the teachable moment by repeating my observation three or four different ways until I was sure I drove the point home thoroughly. All you thick -headed guys need to read this paragraph two or three times to make sure you understand what valuing a woman means.

Girl Wisdom

There is much to be learned from listening. I asked about ten different single girls what they saw in married couples that they really admired. Being valued was on the top of their list, and all of them said that does NOT mean buying flowers or opening the car door. Each of the girls wanted to be a key member of the team. They wanted to be more than a pretty china doll. They all hated the idea of being relegated to mere kitchen help and cleaning lady. Every one of the girls wanted to be actively involved in helping their husbands make a living or run a business; they wanted to share in the decision-making regarding the household. Basically, all the girls wanted a rewarding life. Don't you? My own wife of forty-plus years says this is the number-one important issue in her life. She has often stopped what she was doing and simply thanked me for allowing her the opportunity to use her gifts and talents to the maximum. The word you need to take note of is *opportunity*.

Many—maybe even most—husbands are very glad for their wives to get a job or do some kind of project to make a little money. This is not what I am talking about. A wife getting a job will have negative repercussions. As a matter of fact, if she has a job, she will be giving her help to someone else, and you can see where that might go. That is doing the exact opposite of Scripture. The opportunity to be part of your team is what your wife will cherish. Being part of YOUR team means sharing some kind of business or project that can be done as a team—team, meaning her working with you.

For example: At one time couples ran farms as a team. Every day each aspect of the farm would be discussed and the chores would be divided. The woman knew what her husband was doing, and he knew her chores, so at the end of the day they, as a team, could compare notes and help each other as needed. It is the way things were meant to be. Farmers have the lowest divorce rate of any vocation, and they live the longest. Too bad we can't all be farmers.

> *If your wife doesn't feel like you need her, then YOU are failing in your job.*

During my forty-something years of marriage, I have been a pastor, professional artist, sign painter, cabinet maker, organic vegetable farmer, rock layer, welder, and author, as well as several other odd occupations. I always needed my wife to help me be a success at my occupation. The more I needed her, the better she liked it, as long as I did more than my share of the work. When she was needed more in the business, I didn't misuse her (well, maybe a little) but took more of the home-front responsibilities. When I was a pastor, she learned to counsel. When I made my living as an artist, she painted pictures and ended up selling as much as I did. Even though she was homeschooling five children, I often took her on the job to help hang the signs. When I was an organic vegetable farmer, the whole family was involved. When I wrote my first book, she was the one who investigated the publishing industry. Our first, small, self-published book took the homeschool world by storm because of her marketing skills. Then she started writing, because I needed her to do so. I have needed her to do and be a lot, and she has risen to every challenge because I valued her ability, opinion, and skills.

> *When you lead your new wife down the lane of making you happy, healthy, and wealthy, you are not going to have a bored wife.*

Women see their worth in different areas. My wife's worth came in her ability to work alongside me as an equal. Some women need to know they are good hostesses; others need to find worth in their husband's appreciation for their cooking and decorating skills. Men find self-worth at the job or in sports. A woman's self-worth is tied up in how she is performing as a wife. She was created to be a help meet, and it is in this capacity that she finds fulfillment. She was created to HELP her man, and if she is not doing so in a real and meaningful way, she will be unfulfilled as a human being and dissatisfied with the marriage relationship.

It is a man's responsibility to discover his wife's gifts and what she can do that will make her feel a sense of participation and accomplishment. A lot of her fulfillment will come through assisting you in your vocation. It will take a few months of marriage for her to develop her value system and for you to discern ways she can make you a success. As she comes to understand the varied aspects of your work, she will discover a vacuum and try to fill it. It could be your bookkeeping that needs a little organization, or customer relationships, or purchasing, or research, or any number of ways she thinks she can facilitate your success. Encourage her to leap into the seat beside you and do what she can. It's foreplay. Not that sex is our primary focus, but I can assure you that it is the barometer of how well we are satisfying our little lady. A

When a Mr. Steady is active in helping those with gifts of teaching and preaching make wise decisions, then everyone will be blessed.

woman who doesn't feel treasured during the long days of drudgery cannot be made to feel treasured during the brief bouts of booty bouncing.

Today, right now, as an unmarried man, you need to develop a mindset that when you do take a wife, you will welcome her to walk beside you, not behind you, and certainly not sit on the sidelines.

Not being a doctor or a lawyer, I have no idea what a wife could do to help a man in those fields, but I do know that to have a truly successful marriage, your wife needs to be a very important part of your team. I have noticed that most doctors are too busy, thus terribly behind on the latest research. So I would think that a wife could be her husband's research assistant. He could discuss difficult cases with her and she could search out a treatment. She needs to be the MOST important part of your team. You need to listen to her ideas and consider the viability of them. You need to discuss your work and your vision to improve the field of medicine and care of the patient. Very few men ever make it to the top of anything without a helper, and those that do make it to the top are not balanced or loved. And no helper will ever be more loyal than a loved wife.

Plan Ahead

Decide now that you will plan your life around working together as a team. Once you meet a girl you think you could like, don't just court her; get to know her mind. What are her convictions concerning raising children? Read books and discuss the issues. Ask her what kind of small venture she has to make money. Share your ideas on how she could increase her productiveness and satisfaction. Her response will tell you a lot about the girl and her attitude. Don't forget to walk off and leave her if the occasion calls for walking. Read through marriage books and the Scripture concerning marriage and discuss it with her. Find out what she thinks, because if you don't there will be issues ahead that would weigh down your marriage.

Watch What You Watch

A woman needs affirmation that you think she is more physically attractive than other women. Remember, she is a help meet; in that role she needs to feel that SHE and she alone will meet your romantic and sexual needs. She must be the fulfillment of all your fantasies. The eye food you now consume will affect her after you are married. If a young woman knows you watch doubtful movies or play video games with big-busted babes,

Spend your first year helping just her or taking her along every time you feel you have to help someone else, and things will be better.

or worse, view porn, then you are robbing her of the possibility of feeling special. Furthermore, you are making it impossible for God to bless you in your relationship with your future wife. There are some things in life that have eternal consequences no matter how loud or often you repent.

As a single guy, it is difficult for you to believe this, but every woman has ups and downs, especially when she is pregnant or in the first few months after a baby, and this roller coaster of emotions will cause her to doubt whether you think she is beautiful.

Every young man should make a list of things he will remember when he is married: If she is fat, tell her skinny women look sick. If she is tall, tell her she reminds you of a real hot jungle woman. Just tell her she is your babe and no other will ever take you to places she takes you. But no matter what you say, a man can steal his wife's future self-assurance by looking at other females online or in public. If you have a habit of doing this now, it will carry over into the future. Being married does not heal the soul, and your soul is corrupt if you view pornography. When you steal your wife's confidence in this area, you are intentionally destroying your happiness, sexual fulfillment, and success in marriage.

Now Back to the Priestly/Steady Man

Most of you Steady men are going to marry Go-to girls who are a little bossy and know-it-all. How can I know that? Because the lady who pushes herself into your life and helps you make that fateful decision is the one you will go with, and that will surely be a Go-to girl. You have a tendency to like this type of female. Maybe it answers the vacuum that you experience from being so steady and even-keeled. She brings the excitement you can not force yourself to produce alone. If your friends have an opportunity to give you advice, they will think you are crazy. A Command man will not like a bossy female and will tell you that you are messing with a powder keg. A Visionary man will like her a little, but will prefer a girl who has more Servant in her.

If she doesn't feel that she is successful, then YOU are failing in your job.

If you are wise, you will exercise a great deal of discretion and wait for that girl that seeks the LORD and understands the scriptural exhortation for her to honor and obey her husband. That knowledge will cause her to do the right thing even if she has a mind of her own. YOU NEED to do your homework, because a Go-to girl will choose YOU someday. You need to develop enough backbone to frown her down if you determine she is not the girl for you. The chapter "The International Dilemma" is the love story of a really nice Mr. Steady man who had three Go-to girls after him. He got the gold. Follow his example.

In Conclusion

When you do marry, your job will be to make allowances for your bride so that she feels that what she is doing makes you (1) happier, (2) healthier, and (3) wealthier. The important part of the previous sentence is "feels that." If she doesn't feel that she is successful, then YOU are failing in your job.

Happier

Your new wife will need to believe she makes you happy, that she pleases you in all that she is. In order for her to believe it to be true, she needs to see, feel, and experience your appreciation. Again, you will never convince her of your sincere love with sexual moves. She needs to feel that you love her soul and mind as well as her body. Most men only know how to show appreciation for the body, and that is no deeper than a dog's drive. Your love for her body only means you have a woman available, and she knows it. A woman loves to feel that her husband is terribly in love—not just in love, but terribly in love.

Mr. Steady men are critical to keeping harmony and helping make wise decisions.

Compliments, "thank you," and "I love you" will help build her up, but even that needs to be an outflowing of your soul rather than just an expression of good manners or a form of manipulation.

Healthier

The second area in which you need to encourage her to focus is the health of the family. Get her started early learning good nutrition, and the entire family will be blessed. When a wife learns to cook in a healthy manner, it saves money on eating out, on dentists, and on doctors. She might learn gardening, herbs, juicing, and the role of exercise in keeping the family healthy. This is school for a new wife—"wife school" instead of homeschool. Let her know what you hope she will learn. Show an interest and be willing to try her new, healthy foods. This could make or break your family.

Wealthier

The third way she can help is to make you wealthier! In case you didn't notice, this goes back to a woman needing to be valued. Proverbs 31 is written by a mother to her son, giving him advice on how to choose a wife—a wife who will in some way make him wealthier. If you are not familiar with that passage, then stop and read it. God thought her advice was good enough to include it in his written Word, so you would be wise to get to know the passage. Chapter 16 explores this passage.

As a single man, you need to know that if a girl is sitting on her butt at home doing nothing to advance herself, she is not your Proverbs 31 gal. A girl who is pouring all her energies into sports or some other transient project is not your gal. You need a girl who is already running the mature race so that all you need do is direct her energies toward a path that will bless the family. Start gently directing her now while you are getting to know her, and it will allow you to see how she responds to your encouragement and direction.

When you lead your new wife down the lane of making you happy, healthy, and wealthy, you are not going to have a bored wife. As a married man, you are not your own; your lady has reins on you just as you have reins on her. The following passage refers to sex, but the principle applies here as well. God says, **"Let the husband render unto the wife due benevolence: and likewise also the wife unto the husband. The wife hath not power of her own body, but the husband: and likewise also the husband hath not power of his own body, but the wife."** 1 Corinthians 7:3-4 Life is give, not take; it is pouring into another, and only then will it splash back and bless you. The more you pour, the more you receive. Trust me; I know.

Leaders Need You

Married or unmarried, you are a very necessary brother in the body of Christ. If you are a Mr. Steady, you probably will not see yourself as a leader. But in business, community, and the church, Mr. Steady men are critical to keeping harmony and helping make wise decisions. I have always been in the role of leader, and have been held in esteem for my gifts, but I have needed dependable men who are slow and thoughtful to help in my ministry. There have been times when I have acted rashly, but a fellow brother who would never preach or teach gave a simple word

> *God created her to be a help meet, a person made to help you do what needs to be done.*

of caution that helped me see a clearer picture. The Bible speaks of this: **"If then ye have judgments of things pertaining to this life, set them to judge who are least esteemed in the church."** 1 Corinthians 6:4 Mr. Steady men often don't consider the value of their judgment, but God clearly sets the matter before us when he concludes, **"I speak to your shame. Is it so, that there is not a wise man among you? No, not one that shall be able to judge between his brethren?"** 1 Corinthians 6:5

When a Prophet/Visionary is called in to help make a judgment, it can result in emotional conflict, and nothing wise will come of the matter. If a King/Command man is called in, then his way is final, so there is no choice between options. The men whom God says should help make weighty decisions are men who have not been pushed to the front by their gifts. Priest/Steady men need to be of service to the church in this regard. When a Mr. Steady is active in helping those with gifts of teaching and preaching make wise decisions,

Believe it or not, if you really love a woman— truly value her—and show her how to grow as a human being, she will want to serve you.

then everyone will be blessed. It is the service of the three kinds of men together that causes a church to have balance. The men with the leadership roles do their part and the Mr. Steady men must do theirs as well.

Think of all your friends and you will notice that the vast majority of men are Steady. They are the bedrock of any society. They are the salt of the earth. As a Steady man, you enjoy visiting with folks, and, more importantly, folks enjoy visiting with you. The problem with the Steady guy is that you like to talk and visit on a superficial level; but when it comes to serious, intimate conversation with your new bride, you just don't know what to say, so you don't say much. The same thing happens at church. You get extremely emotional if you try to share anything at church, and since you don't want to break down and cry, you just don't speak. At church there is always someone else to yak, but at home with the wife, you are the only man around. Your wife will need you to speak your mind. This is a weakness in you, so you need to know NOW that talking, teaching, and instructing your new bride is necessary in order for her to grow and for your marriage to flourish. At the back of this book is a seven-lesson guide that you need to work through with your lady. It is a good start.

Mr. Popular

One advantage you have over the other types of men is that people will like you. As a Steady guy, you are always in demand because you are a willing helper. People will feel free to call on you to fix their computer, pick them up when their car breaks down, or help them out of a jam. You need to remember that the lady in your life has first dibs on you. You will forget, and she will get her feelings hurt, and you will say you will try to do better. Spend your first year of marriage helping her or taking her along every time you feel you have to help someone else.

> *Women who are appreciated have a desire to please the person who appreciates them.*

Most young girls are dazzled by Mr. Command and often swoon over the crazy Mr. Visionary. It is the thrill that draws the girls. So don't be surprised when some stuck-on-himself, arrogant, over-stuffed jerk, or some skinny, fussy-haired joker draws more female attention than you do. Stick around; once girls get past the teenybopper stage and mature into young women, they begin to prefer Mr. Steady. As a woman matures, she starts thinking about the baby carriage, which prompts a need for security. Sorry, Mr. Visionary, I would suggest you marry a younger girl, because an older girl will not be so tolerant of, nor will she appreciate, your wild ideas. Mr. Command, you should consider a younger wife too, since older girls will not like your bossy, selfish ways. (Although when you marry young girls you might get yourself in trouble because you never know how a young girl is going to turn out.) Mr. Steady, you do have some things going your way. You can have a more mature bride who has proven herself to be a worthy pick. But when you marry, you have your work cut out for you.

> *It takes all three images of God working in a man to bring about good stability.*

Be Who You Are

Steady Amish Boys

Some of you, like my sons, were born into a good home where your daddy and older brothers were created in an image different from you, so you grew up influenced by a broader expression of our human natures. From your youth it made you more balanced, but it may be more difficult to discern your image. Among the Amish, the image of Priest/Steady is highly valued and considered more spiritual. This image appears more humble, so all the Amish men have tried to adopt the air of the Steady/Priestly man. Their community life is very much communal and depends upon surrender to the corporate will, so a Command man or a radical Visionary is a detriment to the long term preaching and tradition perpetuated from one generation the next. There is no place for change. The Steady man in his servant, priestly expressions is the perfect fit for the status quo.

At first I thought the gentle nature in the Amish must be genetic. But when we got to know the different young men and watched them grow up, we saw there in the recesses of their personalities their true images seeking to find expression. The Command or Visionary was hidden behind a curtain of Steady, and they thought poorly of themselves for the impulses they suppressed. It is an interesting laboratory observing that these men were able to suppress their natures. They carefully control themselves, spending their lives second-guessing their motives? They come to value the diminishing of their God-given natures, but to what end? Do they win the lost to Christ? Do they see prostitutes come to forgiveness? Of what eternal value is their fruit? It is of value to the tranquility and perpetuation of the community but not to a lost and dying world. **"And he said unto them, Go ye into all the world, and preach the gospel to every creature."** Mark 16:15 God needs all three types of men. Be glad for the man God created you to be.

TIME TO CONSIDER:

Here's a MUST-DO list for Mr. Steady in preparing for a wife:

- Create a Proverbs 31 list of ideas for your future bride.

- Don't be a tail-tucker, letting her rule and reign. Start asserting yourself now in relationships, work, games, and at church.

- Be ready to judge in the church when you are needed. Start now and practice so you will be ready.

- Open your heart, soul, and mind to your lady of choice. Learn to talk to her about weighty things. Make a list of things you will talk about, and then make yourself do it.

- Make a commitment to talk to her first, second, and third, with others after that. Make yourself a note in your notebook.

- Think about things you can do to be romantic so that when you marry you will be conditioned to doing them regularly. A list in your notebook might help. Ask some married ladies to give you ideas. Some guys are just naturally romantic; don't think you are one of them.

It takes Priestly/Steady men and Prophet/Visionary men working along with King/Command men to make a church a good mix that is able to function in a way that will bless all.

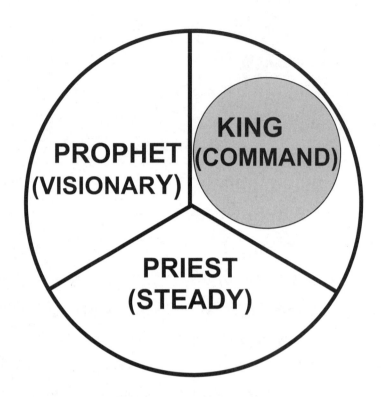

The Three Male Images

Some men are dominant, strong, commanding, and powerful in leadership and strength, reflecting God the Father, the King of Glory.

Chapter 10

KING/MR. COMMAND

God is sovereign, all-powerful. He said, **"Let us make man in our image."** God the Father, God the Son, and God the Holy Spirit counseled together to create finite man in their image. And so he/they did. One man reflects the Holy Spirit: a Prophet/Visionary who is compelled to call others to perfection. Another man is kind and longsuffering, reflecting the Savior, Christ the Lord. This man is steady and dependable. He is priestly. And yet other men are dominant, strong, commanding, and powerful in leadership and strength, reflecting God the Father, the King of Glory. We have discussed the Prophet/Visionary and the Priest/Steady man. Now we will discuss the King/Command image.

A few men are born with more than their share of command—a readiness to step to the front and lead those who dawdle without direction. They are recognized for their presence and are often put in places of leadership, or they make their own way to positions that command others. Most leaders are born, not made. They are created from the womb, but life hones them to a useful edge or grinds them down to frustration and failure.

A few men in history stand out as pure commanders: Washington, Patton, Hitler, and one of my favorites, Churchill. This type of man can be an asset or an ass; no other word can accurately describe how others feel about him. Being a strong leader doesn't mean his ideas are right, holy, or just; he just leads people the way he wants them to go. This leader can have noble ends and bring about a nation, or he can go down in infamy on the bodies of those he has trampled. There is no virtue in one's natural type, only in the use he makes of it.

Throughout history leaders of this type have surrounded themselves with strong men to help get big jobs completed.

If you will learn to think of your wife's pain as your own, you will change your way of thinking and how you treat your coming bride.

King/Command men often do more than is required of them. When committed to the welfare of the masses, they serve the world with honor. To have the nature and opportunity to organize others to great ends is a demanding responsibility and a terrible burden at the same time.

If you are one of these men, I pity your poor wife, because you will expect her to wait on you hand and foot. I know this type well, for I am one, although I have the wild hair of the Visionary as well. My wife could write books for you commanding fellows, since she has spent her life serving one. She is a Servant/Steady girl, willing to lay down her life in service to me, except for a small streak of wild Visionary she shows now and again. As a couple working in complete harmony together, we are able to manifest all three types, and have accomplished much together.

As a King/Command type, I do not mean to be bossy; it's just a part of my nature. I tell

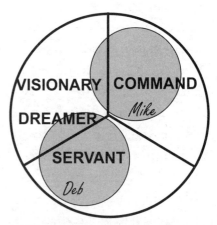

A good balance, representing all three images.

her what to do, how to do it, and when to do it, and she does as I say…usually. Amazing, wonderful, and convenient…for me, anyway.

Believe it or not, if you really love a woman—truly value her—and show her how to grow as a human being, she will want to serve you. God created her to be a help meet, a person made to help you do what needs to be done. Just as I was created with an image meant to command, she was created to be a helper. It is her nature, and she will want to do what is naturally a part of her. The trick is to treat her as you would have others treat you, and then you get this wonderful service. That is a hard feat to perform. No man ever constantly puts others first, Mr. Command least of all.

Love is when you are more attuned to her joy than your success.

If you are a Command man, as you mature you will develop some strengths, but the strengths can also become serious flaws if they are not moderated by wisdom and discretion. Like a gifted athlete, your confidence in your strengths may lead you to think you can defy the rules that govern weaker, less capable mortals. So my exhortation to you is more like the first precept for medical doctors—"First, do no harm." If you learn to use your strengths solely for the good of others, without spending people like currency in the process, you will be a very wise man indeed.

I can best describe the nature of a Command man (King type) by looking at him as a married man. That is the context in which his strengths and weaknesses will most readily manifest themselves for good or ill. Just knowing ahead of time the issues you will face in marriage, and how you might respond to different types of girls, will aid you in discerning the type that will best suit you.

Defrauding Blackmail

A Command man is prone to lack tolerance in every facet of life. His intolerance will prompt him to more quickly walk off and leave a clamoring wife, never considering the possibility that his unyielding and insensitive shell may have driven her to extreme emotional and erratic behavior. Most people yell when someone tramples on them. As a Command man, you are proud of your honest firmness, but you need to regard the fact that your firm stand may be putting harmful pressure on your weaker vessel—your wife. You have a tendency to be neither intimate nor vulnerable; you see no need to share your personal feelings. Because this is already a propensity for you, you will tend to close down emotionally as a way of controlling your wife. This one thing could make or break her—and you. Where Mr. Steady might not talk to his honey because he doesn't know what to say, you will refuse to communicate with her out of pride that she has no right to challenge you, or as a way of controlling her. Being a Command man doesn't save you from being stupid, and it doesn't obligate anyone to follow you or even respect you.

When a man does not communicate with his lady in a normal way, or if he uses silence to control her behavior, it can make a good woman feel terribly shut out. A woman can live in a cave on little food and still be faithful, but she will not survive being defrauded physically, mentally, or emotionally. Often a Command man will be fool enough to think he can control his wife's behavior by not talking with her or by declining to touch her. Few Command men call it punishing; they say they are just getting the wife in line, waiting for her to get her head straight. Dictatorship does not a happy marriage make.

The will to dominate mars any relationship, and the inclination to dominate is in all of us. It destroys marriages.

On the positive side, a humble Command man (almost an oxymoron) is of service to mankind. There are many people with talents and gifts who lack the gumption to step forward and serve.

The Command personality does not have to be accomplished in a field to see the need for leadership and volunteer his services. When there is a house fire or an auto accident, while others stand around wondering why someone doesn't do something, the Command man steps forward and starts giving orders, organizing the bystanders into an emergence rescue team.

You only rise as high as you lift your wife.

In the home, the Command man will organize the wife and kids into a cohesive team and get things done. At church, he sees a need and steps to the mic to tell everyone what to do. He expects people to jump when he speaks. He may have little patience with inaction and hesitation. Surprisingly, studies have shown that daughters raise by commanding fathers, even the overbearing ones, are more likely to be secure and accomplished—loving and respecting their fathers to a higher degree. An emotionally stable Command man brings a sense of security to a family, leaving everyone with a feeling that there is someone in charge and all is well.

Love is when she hurts and you stop everything to make her well.

Recipe for Failure

What happens when an immature Command man marries an immature Go-to gal? Right now as I write, I am reminded of a man who has a great deal of talent and could go far in his field of expertise. His wife is brilliant—a little stubborn, maybe even rebellious, but bubbling with creativity. All he sees is her rebellion, and his single response is to shut down toward her. So he maintains emotional distance as a way of showing his disdain for her stubbornness. She feels it as his way of punishing her, and she stays mad all the time. To add to their misery, because both of them are commanding in nature, they maintain an attitude of "my way or the highway." Thankfully they don't believe in divorce, but unless they humble themselves and start loving, honoring, and doing what is right for each other, they will never be happy or productive as a couple, AND they will eventually have all they can take and divorce anyway.

Divorce never just happens; it comes in increments, daily making decisions to love one's self and protect one's pride rather than love **"as Christ also loved the church, and gave himself for it."** Ephesians 5:25

> *When a man is wise and sees his wife as his helper rather than his competitor, he can release her gifts to propel them both to success.*

We are all shocked when we hear that some wonderful, older couple has announced that they are divorcing, but don't let their public life fool you. For more years than they can remember, that older couple has been actively hating each other, baiting each other, and living so as to cause grief instead of glory. Divorce starts early; some folks just jump off the sinking boat sooner than others. Don't let it happen to you.

Back to our story of the two commanding hardheads. Regardless of good counsel to the contrary, he has maintained an adversarial attitude toward her since the day they were married. What he needs to do is break the cycle of pride and offense and ask her to help him in achieving his vocational goals. He needs to stop controlling and allow her some latitude in exercising her discretion in executing her vision for advancing him in his field. Even if she fails, his appreciation for her trying will make the marriage succeed. She is fully capable—actually smarter than he is—and he would benefit if he would only give her opportunity and a little praise. She might still be somewhat ornery, as is he, but working WITH him would give her a sense of fulfillment and greatly improve her attitude. Women who are appreciated have a desire to please the person who appreciates them. Anyone who is treated with disregard or, worse yet, ignored will never want to please their persecutor. If this husband would get off his high horse and just learn to let her HELP him, she would meet his needs and he could quit his 8-to-5 job and make more money more easily while doing what he loves.

You Need Her Help

God gave Adam a helper. He is to love her as his own flesh. When she is sick, he should care for her as he would be cared for. When she is weak, he is to hold her up. This does not come naturally to a Command man. To be the kind, loving, sacrificial man requires constant attentiveness to her needs contrary to his natural inclinations.

As a Command man, being sufficient unto yourself is both a strength and weakness. It is what allows you to take the burden of command. A commander has to do what is best for the largest number, and that often means personal sacrifice. It means bearing the criticism of many, knowing that what they say is partly true, but knowing you have acted for the common good. Most men can't take the condemnation and still sleep at night. There are times when being a man of authority is interpreted as pride by those looking on, and that is a burden most men would gladly lay down.

It takes all three images of God working in a man to bring about good stability.

You may be a Command man, but you are also the husband of a wife who has needs, and she is your first priority. Adam declared that Eve was bone of his bone. **"One flesh"** perfectly describes what God intends a marriage to be. It is caring and working toward the same goals. In speaking of marriage God said, **"So ought men to love their wives as their own bodies. He that loveth his wife loveth himself. For no man ever yet hated his own flesh; but nourisheth and cherisheth it, even as the Lord the church."** Ephesians 5:28-29

If all husbands obeyed that one verse, marriage would be a paradise instead of the subject of endless self-healing books. If you will learn to think of your wife's pain as your own, it will be the ground of a happy and productive marriage.

The Balance

As a Command man there have been times when I thought I could see a situation clearly and there was no need to listen to the

The more you need, the greater will be her need to help.

opinion of anyone else. Other opinions, my wife's included, were a waste of time. But time and circumstances have mellowed me. My hair is white, my beard is long and thin, and my back is bent by the years.

And, yes, age has dimmed my natural vision, but it has also given me eyes that see clearer than ever before. I am not so encumbered by an overload of testosterone that it distorts my thoughts. Now, I know all Command men need constant advice to balance them. It takes all three images of God working in a man to bring about good stability. It takes Priestly/Steady men and Prophet/Visionary men working along with King/Command men to make a church a good mix that is able to function as the bride of Christ.

A well-rounded man will understand the need to develop expressions of the image types different from his. A lazy, selfish man is content to follow the line of least resistance and just do what comes naturally without regard for the need of a more rounded approach.

If you are a Steady man who is uncomfortable taking the lead, yet you see the need, especially in your family, you are morally obligated to lead regardless of how it makes you feel. If a Command man is wise he will see that there are times when he needs to defer leadership to others and function as a follower. Likewise, there are times when the moment calls for a priestly response and the Command man is the only one in a position to respond. If he falls back into his comfort zone, the priestly ministry will go unanswered and someone will suffer—maybe his wife. If a man is a Visionary, he should stop to visit the sick and help the old lady with her plumbing. And if he is a Command man, he should occasionally clean the church building and help wash the dishes after the church dinner. We need to develop those things in ourselves that will bring us balance.

The Command Pastor Who Shuts the Eternal Door

As men of God doing the work of God, we need balance. The more we are open to understand the images of other men, both their strengths and weaknesses, and are willing to make allowances for the differences, the more effectively we can organize others to productive ends. As I sit typing, I am reminded of a good pastor of a fine Bible-believing church. He is a Command man. In his congregation is a gentle Steady/Visionary who has a true vision for reaching the lost. His approach is gentle, less confrontational, but effective. With his Go-to/Dreamer wife at his side, they are dedicated to going into the highways and byways, spending their own money to take the gospel to the lost. For years before the present pastor came to their church, they were active in full-time evangelism, and they bore glorious fruit. Sadly, the pastor doesn't count their fruit worthwhile; he is only interested in the numbers that fill the pews. The pastor struggles with trying to control them because he feels they are not on board with what the church is doing. There is a constant power struggle that leaves this Steady missionary couple feeling out of order in their need to minister to the lost.

The Command pastor will either lose this family or strip away their calling. In either case, he will wind up trembling at the Judgment Seat of Christ, having to give an answer as to why he commanded contrary to the will of God. Either way he is pulling down the church because he tries to maintain control. I would ask this pastor: Why are you so certain that any ministry to the lost must be focused on adding to the membership of "your" church?

Little Command Men

I turn the other way and laugh when I see young Command boys trying to act like experienced men. It seems that age and wisdom have little to do with the feelings of command. I have seen inept and inexperienced young men start bossing everybody around as if they were in charge and were God's gift to disorganization and inaction. The immature Command boy is driven to take control even when he has no idea which direction the ship should be steered. A gift of nature is not a license to act upon impulse. The desire to command is not the same as the wisdom to command. The ability to command is not authority to command. Hard lessons to learn. Failure is usually the only cure. Until a man distrusts himself and, in particular, his natural impulses, he is not qualified to lead anyone else.

The desire to command is not the same as the wisdom to command.

Command men are often treated with esteem, and it can really go to a man's head. He can begin to feel superior simply because of his God-given nature. God reminds us **"unto whomsoever much is given, of him shall be much required: and to whom men have committed much, of him they will ask the more."** Luke 12:48

Slave or Lover

Mr. Command men are attracted to Servant/Steady girls. They want their ladies to stand ready to wait on them. If you are a Command man, you will fight to the death (figure of speech, hopefully) if you marry a hardheaded Go-to girl. If you are a fool you will squash the talent right out of a Dreamer/Visionary girl. A Command man meets the least resistance married to a girl who loves to serve. These girls are easy to spot. They are the ones always busy helping others. They like to help cook for crowds, and clean-up is their specialty. They will jump anytime someone needs help setting up a room for a meeting or be ready to take in a sick puppy. They are the givers, doers, helpers, and encouragers. They usually smile a lot and are cheerful. It makes me smile just thinking of these girls.

If her flesh is treated like a slave, then a part of you is a slave and will rise no further than that.

They are like honey. For Mr. Steady they are sticky-sweet and maybe a little too much. Mr. Visionary will like them but not really be attracted to them. Servant/Steady girls were created for Command men. Woe to you men who misuse them, for there will be a judgment, and I suspect that many Command men will cringe when the way they treated their little honeys is brought to light.

How High Will You Rise?

When you marry, your wife will want to please you. It is in her nature. You need to remember that you want a friend and lover, not a slave. It is easy to use her because she will be willing as long as you show appreciation. She is flesh of your flesh. If her flesh is treated like a slave, then a part of you is a slave and will rise no further. You only rise as high as you lift your wife. But if you lift her up and cause her to stand with you—if you serve her as she serves you—then you will have a lover equal to yourself. Until she

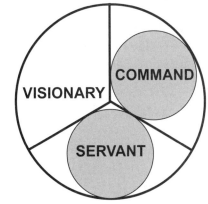

A Command man and a Servant lady make a good balance.

is there with you, you will never rise to where you could have gone.

In my mind I can think of so many men who never made it in ministry, or life for that matter. They wanted so much for their children to grow up in honor and be preachers or teachers. They tried so hard to make it happen, homeschooling, going to church five times a week, and all the things a

You are tethered to her success as a person.

man does to succeed. I can also see younger men who are following in the same footsteps of folly. These men think they can be successful in spite of their relationship to their wives. They believe she drags her feet, or is weak, and is at best a hindrance. You know families like this, and maybe you have agreed with the man. Where the fault lies doesn't matter; the fact remains that as a married man he is one flesh with that lady; he is yoked with her in life, and where she is, he will remain. He is tethered to her success as a person.

All She Needs

Divorce destroys God's plan. If a man wants to go far, he needs her pulling with him—they need to be pulling together. A man will be wise to remember that she is his flesh and that he loves his own flesh; he cherishes it and protects it and nourishes it. So if she is hurting in any way, he should stop all activity until his flesh is restored to health and joy. He can't bully his flesh to be healed, and he can't starve his flesh to bring healing; he can't command, ignore, or even beg. It takes a loving hand of healing to bring a wife to the place of growth and joy. And when a man chooses to lay aside his own aspirations in order to mature his wife, she will be thankful and know that she is loved. All a woman truly wants is a man to love her. A man finds this hard to understand. Men are driven to succeed, to master, to create, to command, to see a thing through, and to make things happen. Women were created to help us, and they only need one thing to keep them fueled: appreciation.

As a young, unmarried man, you find it hard to believe you would ever treat your bride with anything less than tender love. But you will. Now is the time to begin thinking about these things and admitting your possible weaknesses. Being forewarned is being forearmed, ready for the battle to establish a heavenly marriage.

The Conclusion of the Matter

Love is when you are more attuned to her joy than to your success. Love is when you care more about her needs than your own. Love is when you are more concerned with her health than your own. Love is when she hurts and you stop everything to make her well. Love is all she needs. Many men equate love with sex, service, surrender, or affirmation. Those men are destined to be failures, not only in marriage but in life.

> *Love is when you care more about her needs than your own.*

Where Are the Girls?

There are thousands of homeschooled young women at home pining to be brides. They are asking, where are the men? The men are on a construction site digging footings; they are behind a computer setting up the boss's website; they are clerking at Lowe's or at some other business.

So how shall the sexes meet? Good question. The men need to go hunting. You are the hunter, so it is up to you to seek and find. Girls go to missions conferences hoping to meet a good man; they go to homeschool reunions and stand around frustrated because the place is full of girls and very few guys. These poor girls go to church where only a handful of young boys—way too young for them—are available. It's a formula to end posterity. Go hunting. Take note of the next Shindig and make preparation to come shopping.

TIME TO CONSIDER:

Proverbs 16 is full of wisdom.
Make a list of verses that stand out to
you. One verse mentions me. Do you
know which one?

Rooting Out Bitterness

A root of bitterness is subtle, hard to detect, difficult to root out,
and very costly to your future family. You don't want to marry a girl
that springs from a root of bitterness. The sins of the parents do affect
a person. Divorce is the marker of this ugly root and it passes to the
children that suffer through it. The root is often deep and wound
tight. *Forgiveness* is the cleanest, neatest word you will ever know.
Make use of it often.

> **Follow peace with all men, and holiness, without which no
> man will see the Lord: Looking diligently lest any man fail
> of the grace of God; lest any root of bitterness springing
> up trouble you, and thereby many be defiled; Lest there
> be any fornicator, or profane person, as Esau, who for one
> morsel of meat sold his birthright.** Hebrew 12:14-16

A Few More Things

There are seven lessons at the end of this book that you need to work through with your future honey. Even if you have never done a Bible study, you can do these, for they are laid out in a way that is systematic and easy to follow. Teach her from the Word, and have her read my wife's books on marriage, *Preparing to Be a Help Meet* and *Created to Be His Help Meet*. Read along with her those parts that you feel are critical; ask her views and opinions. Read and discuss the Bible passages on marriage, and let her talk about them.

Finally, you will want to be married to a girl who views marriage as an opportunity to bless you. And, hopefully, you want to be married so you can bless her. Do YOU deserve a sweetheart?

You are the hunter, so it is up to you to seek and find.

More Girl Talk . . .

A Lesson on Crying

When my husband and I first got married, neither one of us had any idea how differently we viewed emotions. I guess I should say the expression of emotions.

Growing up in a very emotionally open family, it never occurred to me that my husband might not be used to crying. Between my two sisters and me, my brothers were accustomed to emotional outbursts (aka sobbing hysterically over something seemingly insignificant). My brothers were unfazed by crying, and cheerfully comforted us before heading outside to a calmer environment. I expected my new husband would respond much the same.

My husband grew up with one sister and three brothers, and his mom and sister never cried in front of the boys unless someone had died. He understandably assumed that girls just didn't cry much, since he was rarely confronted with a weeping female.

Imagine his shock when he married me, a highly emotional woman, who felt no need to rein in the emotional storms! It made for quite an eventful first year of marriage.

Guys just need to know that sometimes women cry for absolutely no reason. Crying is a sort of emotional release, and there are times when it just feels good to have a nice, long cry.

My husband just could not accept this at first. He insisted that there had to be something wrong, otherwise I wouldn't be crying. I tried to explain to him that I felt like crying and was just letting it all out. He didn't believe me, and demanded that I tell him what was wrong. Had someone hurt my feelings? Had he done something to upset me? Did I find more mice in the kitchen?

In the midst of a particularly emotional fit of tears, I picked up the phone and called his mother.

"Will you please explain to your son that SOMETIMES women just cry for no reason?!?" I sobbed to her.

Silence.

She asked, "Did you not tell him that?"

"I did! He won't believe me! He thinks there has to be a reason!"

"Oh. His dad thought the same thing when we first married. I'll explain it to him." And she did.

It took him a few days, but he started to believe that, yes, women do just cry for the sake of crying. My older brother kindly explained to him that when a woman is crying, you just give her a hug, buy her some chocolate, and try not to do anything dumb. I think that's pretty good advice.

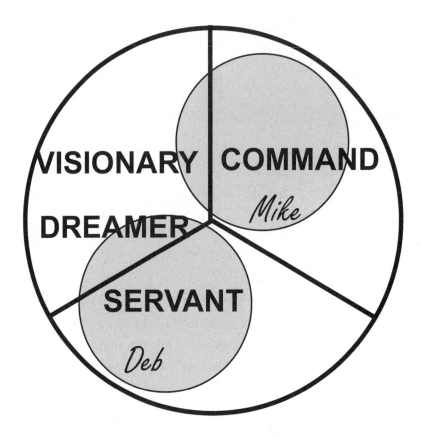

A good balance,
representing all three images

How do we work together?

Chapter 11

MIXING AND MATCHING

I am a King/Command man but I have a lot of Prophet/Visionary in me as well. My wife is a Priestly/Steady/Servant, but she has some of Prophet/Visionary/Dreamer. So how do we work together?

For the first several years of our marriage I saw her gentle Priestly/ Servant traits as very accommodating but not as a foundation for significant contribution to great things. The expressions of her Servant nature seemed immature and weak, for she often caved to strong, dominant, super-spiritual, overbearing females. I stood in disbelief as she back-pedaled the truth to accommodate an aggressive, empty-headed battleaxe. Several times I accused her, "You would lie to avoid confrontation.

Deb and I became a very comfortable dynamic duo, expressing the trio of image types between us.

Why do you let them run over you like that? You have a mind of your own, so speak up." It made me a little angry to see my wife taking nonsense from lesser women. In my Command nature, I am a little like John Wayne: "I don't take nothin' offa nobody." In the ministry there are often conflicts that need to be resolved. She was not able to back me up.

Even in our own family she caved. My mother was and both my sisters are dominant and aggressive. It seems to have run in the family except for my brother, who is the most Priestly/Steady guy you will ever meet. And his wife was the Command/Go-to gal as well. Early in our marriage, we made personal decisions about how we would raise our children and homeschool them. The family just didn't understand us sometimes. I guess I should say, they didn't understand me. I needed my wife to back me up. But in a confrontation she would give ground until she admitted error or ignorance just to please them. It aggravated me to no end. So I made it my mission to build up her confidence and equip her to hold her own in a social setting. It took years before she got her fire burning. But no one runs over her now without getting their feet burned.

She still has her Priestly/Servant nature. I am amazed at her ability to not be offended and to give a soft answer that turns away wrath. I now allow her to run defense for me, because she can take a punch and turn it into a love pat, or she can deliver a counter-blow that ends the fight. Where I am prone to turn a cold shoulder and dismiss my critics, she is able to make friends of them and leave them thinking it was their idea. It is an amazing and wonderful gift. While I am writing you off, she is making a list of ways to win you over. I have always needed that kind of balance, but I didn't realize it was a need until I saw the good fruit she bore over and over again. Together we are much more than we would ever be alone. Together we are whole, and our whole is much greater than the sum of our parts.

Together we are whole, and our whole is much greater than the sum of our parts.

My wife's ability to know things about people without anyone saying anything is remarkable, at least to me. It is because she is sensitive to their spirits; basically she cares about them as people and wants to help them. I want to teach them from Scripture; she wants to help them as people. After all these years of ministering with her, I can clearly see that my way is not a complete package. People just need more than I am able to teach verse by verse. If the contents of this book were left up to me, it would be verse by verse teaching on the book of Romans on how to be free from sin, or a very explicit rendition from the Song of Solomon on how to have sex, and a section on how to avoid bitc…excuse me, how to avoid mean girls and marry a gentle, kind servant girl who will do what you say, when you say it. As you can read in this book, not everything has been left up to me. I have surrendered it to her to edit. She sends it back neutered, and I rewrite it until we are both satisfied that it is what needs to be said.

A confident man can encourage his wife to exercise her gifts and talents and not be intimidated by her success.

I remember seeing a documentary about twin artists who worked for Disney. They worked on projects around the clock. One of them would sleep while the other worked. When the one awoke he took the brush and continued the painting while the other took his turn sleeping. They both said that when they awoke from eight hours sleep and viewed the progress on the painting, they felt as if they had done the work and could continue without a second thought. My wife and I have become a lot like that. We can write a paragraph together and each of us feels that it is our own.

As we got older and our marriage matured, Deb and I became a very comfortable dynamic duo, expressing the trio of image types between us. As we understand our strengths and weakness and defer to the other in those areas where we know we are lacking, both of us have grown to be more balanced in the individual expression of our types. I have become more Steady (Priestly) and she has become more Go-to (Command). And operating in complete cooperation, between us there is a well-rounded reflection of all three types. I contribute the Command and some Visionary and she contributes a significant amount of Servant (Priestly) traits with a little Visionary.

Sons-in-Law

My son-in-law James is a Steady with a lot of Visionary—the same as my wife, but he has an extra dose of the Visionary. When he was single and trying to get into the good graces of my daughter Shoshanna, he would help my wife in the kitchen. I would never have done anything like that. I guess he thought if he could win the mama he would have a better chance at the daughter. He washed more dishes than our dishwasher had ever seen. It could have been that he was scared of me, so he thought Mama Pearl was more approachable. At any rate, he got my girl, and it had nothing to do with the dishes. Come to think of it, he has not volunteered to wash a dish since the day I signed their marriage covenant. I should have written that in the contract.

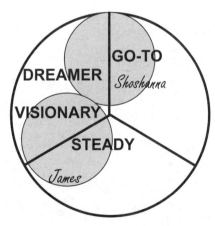

Shoshanna, married to James, is like her father a very commanding Go-to gal with a lot of the Dreamer (Visionary) in her. As a team they are also a dynamic duo, accomplishing more than a whole busload of government workers. As a Command type she likes an audience, and the bigger the better. They have an herb business. She is also beautiful, so she is the face for their business.

She does YouTube videos, creates DVDs, does the advertisements, writes books and magazine articles, and deals with the staff. He manages the technical end, runs the website, comes up with ideas for her to implement, and makes the whole thing hold together. He is the brains behind the whole scene. She is the creativity. She says he gives her wings to fly, and she loves flying. She has no trouble reverencing her man, for he is the critical factor in all her success as a businesswoman and mother. There is no competition between them. They think and work as a team, again, accomplishing more together than either of them could ever do alone. In fact, I can't see either of them being successful alone. Half of an engine will not turn over. Without her, his visions would never find expression, and he would be an inventor trying to invent a useless gadget. Without his Steady side, she would be a disorganized, artistic Visionary with big ideas and no way to accomplish them. Together they are a complete team accomplishing so much it makes me tired just listening to them brainstorm.

Who Wears the Pants?

Many married men will disagree with what I say about releasing a wife's potential, protesting that some women are just bossy and self-promoting, always putting their husbands down, not content unless they are wearing the pants in the family. So, they say, there is no way a husband can allow these women into the command and control room.

Some guys struggle to prove they wear the pants in the family. Most Command and Visionary Men unconsciously hold their wives down so they can "be the man." These

Together they are a complete team accomplishing so much it makes me tired just listening to them brainstorm.

men don't realize that people looking on can clearly see insecure men dominating their weaker vessels in order to appear bigger and better. Let's face it, most men aren't being the man leading the family; they are little boys still trying to win praise and approval by being number one. A confident man can encourage his wife to exercise her gifts and talents and not be intimidated by her success. Rather he can incorporate her abilities into his life endeavors and thereby expand his understanding of the world and increase his ability to act upon it. When a man is wise and sees his wife as his helper rather than his competitor, he can release her gifts to propel them both to success. Balance is so important.

A woman is ready to follow a man who has her best interests at heart.

In a marriage where a weak and lazy Steady man is married to an energetic, confident Go-to gal, she is likely to become frustrated with his slow crawl away from progress. It is the nature of a woman to fill a vacuum. That is what makes them such wonderful help meets. They are like a T-cell, waiting to adapt to where they are needed. They can complete a man. But, being human, they can be ambitions and desirous of success. If they discover that their husbands are dragging their feet or flying off in an impractical direction, or commanding with no clear direction in mind other than maintaining supremacy, they are likely to grab his pants and hat and try to push him out of the captain's chair to save the family from stagnation or, in the case of a radical Visionary, from a high-speed ship wreck.

Weak men band together with a doctrine of female submission in order to keep from having to better themselves.

There are two approaches to avoiding this authority-grabbing woman. One, you can select a help meet who is a Servant girl with little ambition, knowing she will put up with just about anything and, if necessary, suffer in silence. Or you can stir yourself to rise up and seize life with energy and enthusiasm, grabbing your wife by the hand no matter her type and tackle life as a team, employing all the gifts and talents you have between you.

A woman is ready to follow a man who has her best interests at heart. A Go-to gal beaming with energy and vision will follow a Steady man if he encourages her to aid him in his life work. She may even have projects and ministries outside the parameters of his vocation, but not feeling put down by him, she will be thankful for his quiet leading and respect his admirable priestly qualities, knowing she is deficient in that area.

Two humble people of any type, of good character, with fortitude and mercy, can make a good marriage.

A Command man who is weak and autocratic, married to a powerful Go-to gal, is a formula for war. If he commands out of a fear of being diminished or overshadowed by her aggressive nature and he tries to subdue her with a doctrine of submission, she may fight him all the way to the lawyer's. It is unbalanced, dysfunctional marriages like this that cause the preachers to preach all the harder "Wives obey your husbands." Weak men band together with a doctrine of female submission in order to keep from having to better themselves.

God didn't make a mistake when he created help meets. They are ready to help, but they are not content to be forced to silently sit on the bench while you lose the game. So you can better yourself as a man and be able to handle any type of woman, or you can carefully choose a bride who is willing to abide your immaturities with little complaint.

A mature Command man can marry a firebrand Go-to gal/Visionary with no Steady or Servant in the mix, and they will likely be an explosive, hard-driving couple that accomplishes much, but, with their lack of sensitivity, they will hurt a few people along the way.

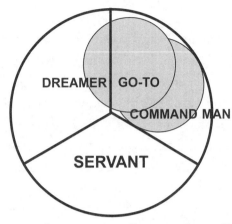

An explosive mix, for good or ill.

Their marriage will be dotted with occasional fights but they will make up with equal vigor. Their success as a team will be found in their double-whammy leadership and drive. Their weakness will be their lack of Priestly qualities.

Ensuring Success

No combination predicts either success or failure. And one's type is not predictive of one's happiness or defeat, good or evil, emotional balance or self-loathing. Character is far more important than your natural type. Two humble people of any type, of good character, with fortitude and mercy, can make a good marriage. The problems to be overcome will differ with the various mixtures of the three types, but after you are married, never blame your marital failure on your types. Problems arise from a failure to make allowance for the differences, but failure is in the heart (immaturity or selfishness), not in natural characteristics.

There is no substitute for wisdom and grace.

We study the different types with their strengths and weaknesses as a way to understand our own motivations and responses and those of our prospective brides and later, wives. It is an observable fact that contrasting types are drawn to each other for it is nature's route to a balanced marriage capable of reflecting all three images. A Steady (Priestly) man will find a Servant (Priestly) woman boring, but will be excited by a Go-to gal. Generally a Command man will not like a commanding Go-to gal, but will find the Servant girl more to his taste. But there is no guarantee that marrying a contrasting type, normally suited to your nature, is going to produce a trouble-free marriage. Selfishness and smallness of spirit are not limited to one combination. There is no substitute for wisdom and grace. No matter what a couple may or may not have in common, if they are heirs together of the grace of

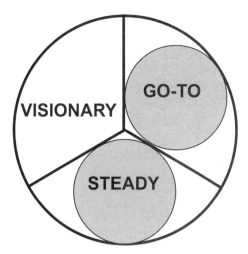

Mr. Steady will find a Go-to gal exciting.

life, they have the foundation for a good marriage. The problems they must work out will differ with the different combinations of image types, but those walking together in grace will come to a happy end.

You can marry a girl who fits you like a glove, but if you fail to bring her alongside you, then you might as well have married a shrew. Marriage is just the beginning of the journey.

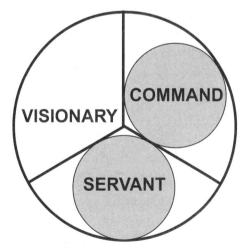

A Command man and a Servant lady make a good balance.

Examples

Right now I know two young couples who are considering marriage. It is so interesting to see how opposites attract.

Couple A

The first couple I'll call the **A's**. Mr. A is a Priestly/ Steady. He is so easy going. He is interested in Miss A who is a Go-to but has a touch of Priestly/Servant. Her assertiveness makes him laugh; she is fun, alive, electric in a way he could never be. She already thinks he is a stick-in-the-mud, but is delighted to be able to delight him. Even as they are

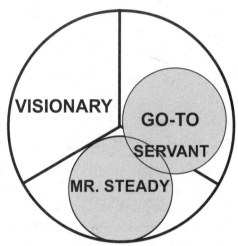

Mr. Steady finds the Go-to/Servant girl to his liking.

considering marriage, she is concerned and hopes that he will allow her to use her gifts and talents to set up shop in her new home.

She likes merchandising. He has a good education and makes plenty of money, so it is possible that he will not understand her need to do something creative as well as lucrative. If he is wise, he will not only allow it, but he will encourage it and help her achieve her goals in a bigger way. Hey, you say, is HE going to be HER help meet? NO, he is developing his help meet to serve them as a couple. He is using her gifts, drives, talents, and type to his advantage. He is loving what she is without trying to force her to be of a different nature. She is going to see him as her savior, the man who makes her fly! And she will be so thankful. Her reverence to him will not be born out of command from Scripture, but from gratitude in her soul. How good is that!

Couple B

I am thinking of another developing couple that is most interesting. They are the **B's**. Mr. B is a Visionary…an unbalanced Visionary, which is to be expected at his age. It is good he is marrying a young girl, for she will need to bend to his peculiarities. Miss B is a Go-to/Command as well as a touch of Servant. They can make a good match in balance. And they will do well IF he listens to his wife's practical advice and IF she appreciates his wild ideas and will believe in his most pressing dreams long enough for him to run some of them to ground even if it means being temporarily bankrupt. He needs to learn that everything he imagines is not necessarily wise, true, or even sane. He can only learn that by trying and failing. If she is there to console him and encourage him to think his visions through a little clearer before committing time and resources, then he will not be broken or bitter, just wiser.

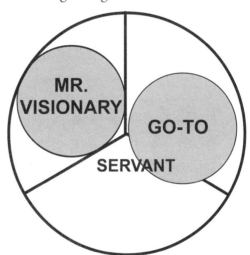

Mr. Visionary and the Go-to gal with a touch of Servant make for a good balance.

A Case of Mistaken Identity

My wife and some other girls were laughing and discussing the men of the church and their natural images, when one of the eighteen-year-old girls spoke up and confidently asserted, "My father is definitely a Command man." When the girls laughed and said, "No, your father is definitely Steady," she laughed and said, "You don't know my father; he commands our house; everybody does what he says." But in reality her father is all Steady with no apparent Command or Visionary. She took him to be a Command man because he does indeed assume the active lead. He has not accepted the natural inclinations of his image type, but has risen to the need and commands where command is needed.

All men should command their homes. God meant for men to be the head of the home regardless of their natural image. Just because a man is of a priestly nature, steady and dependable, serving and compassionate, that doesn't mean he is not capable of taking charge of his home or of the work place. There are many Steady men who are made foremen on a job where they have sixty people working under them. A Steady man may manage the job and workforce quite well. A Steady man may be a pastor and direct a large number of people in church ministries. Likewise, a Command man may be a medical doctor dedicated to serving. A Visionary can command others in a ministry of compassion and healing, though he will be inclined to try new and maybe bizarre methods of getting the job done more effectively.

There are no limitations placed upon us by our natural images.

There are no limitations placed upon us by our natural images. All three images are in each of us in either an understated or overt way. It is true that one of the three will dominate and be obvious to those who know us, but we can and should cultivate the other images within ourselves so that we become a balanced and more productive human expression of the Godhead.

I speak of the ideal. That being said, the fact remains that most people will go though life with a narrow and limited expression of their God-ordained image type. Maturity is the wisdom and self-denial to find balance rather than allowing one's self to simply respond to life in a single dimension. Sometimes commanding is the wrong thing to do. Likewise there are times when it is out of order to be compassionate and stay the course. There are times when the Visionary must lay down his vision and do his daily duty just like a Steady man. There are times when the retiring Steady man must rouse himself from his comfort zone and take charge. He will feel out of place doing so, but wisdom dictates that leadership is what is needed at the moment.

A situation that demands a commanding response will be natural to the Command man but horrifying to the Steady fellow who would rather just focus on his own work and let someone else step forward to lead. Think about this: When the Steady man takes the lead, he is making a sacrifice and is therefore a man of character; whereas when the Command man takes command, he is doing what comes naturally, and since it requires no sacrifice or self-discipline, there is no virtue in his service of leadership. He leads because it feels good. I can say from experience that when there is a need for leadership—a vacuum, you might say—I get anxious and nervous, about to explode, unless I step forward and take over, making everything work for the good of all. It is a personal relief valve to take the lead. It fulfills a need in me to command. Wow! That's humbling.

> *The only true nobility and virtue is found not when we act from the well of our propensities, but when we are compelled to act by our knowledge of the need to serve others—even at our own discomfort.*

Likewise, the Steady man who sees a need for service becomes uncomfortable unless he can throw himself into the mix and serve. He is, in a sense, serving his own need when he serves others— humbling again.

The same principle applies to Visionaries who are responsible for brilliant innovations that bless many. When the Visionary calls men to repentance or throws himself into a campaign for justice, he is taking the only path that will bring satisfaction and rest to his spirit—a self-serving act, though not without merit.

The only true nobility and virtue is found not when we act from the well of our propensities, but when we are compelled to act by our knowledge of the need to serve others—even at our own discomfort. It is that very discomfort and lack of personal satisfaction that makes it a virtue.

Given that men are created in one of three images, a man who spontaneously responds to the circumstances of life from the fountain of his own nature is going to be wrong two-thirds of the time.

What does this have to do with selecting a help meet? If you can better understand yourself, your strengths, and your weaknesses, you can predict the direction of your future growth—know who and what you will be as a married man. Understanding the expressions of the three types will also enable you to understand the gal you are considering and the manner in which the two of you can relate. Furthermore, knowing our weaknesses, we can give attention to rousing ourselves to do what we ought rather than what comes natural.

Moreover, when you are shopping for a wife, know that she is not limited by her image type. If you expect to be a versatile fellow, grabbing life by the horns and making things happen, you will want to

Maturity is having the wisdom and self-denial to find balance in responding to life.

marry a gal who does not accept the limitations of her natural type but is willing to go beyond her propensities and broaden herself into three-dimensional expression. Beginning marriage with a mixture of the three types will give you a head start on being well rounded, but know that complete multi-image expression is possible in any individual and couple regardless of their natural image.

TIME TO CONSIDER:

Ephesians chapter 5 is the chapter
referenced most often concerning marriage.
It is really a life chapter, starting with a
man's walk with the Lord, continuing with his relationship with
people, his use of time, how to worship and work, and finally how a
man is to teach, love, and cherish his wife. The last four words speak
to a wife about reverencing her husband.

Look up this passage in the Bible and outline it. Divide it up into
subjects, and notice the verses that sum up its major points. When
you have a wife, come back and teach it to her, using the outline you
create.

*Husbands, love your
wives, even as Christ
also loved the church,
and gave himself for it.*
Ephesians 5:25

*Confidence in an unfaithful man
in time of trouble is like a broken
tooth, and a foot out of joint.*

Proverbs 25:19

Chapter 12

THE INTERNATIONAL DILEMMA

Remember what I told you about Mr. Steady? I said he would be pursued, usually by older girls who considered him a safe and comfortable domestic partner. For that reason Mr. Steady must be ready to turn the wrong ones down and say yes to the good one.

The following story is about a guy who spent his youth with NO girls interested in him at ALL until he showed up at Bible college. There his most wonderful fantasy came true…or maybe it was a nightmare. Suddenly, more girls wanted him than he could shake a stick at, and how was he supposed to decide? Good problems happen to those who pray. Here's his story told his way.

A Godly Wife: Finding God's Choice

A man's rite of passage, taking a wife, can be an intimidating and often frustrating task. The good news for Bible believers is that her worth far outweighs the effort you must put into finding her. My experience in finding a wife was that God does indeed answer prayer, and he is equally concerned that our brides get as good a deal as we do. Remembering all the foreboding uncertainty associated with the process, I have some advice for those men who want more than just an ordinary marriage.

My story began with a prayer, well, actually with many prayers and loads of worry. But I am confident now that God heard me the first time and that all the anguish and hand wringing only clouded my judgment. It was my desire to find God's choice, but after much searching, I was no closer to finding my soul mate.

During my days in high school and college, I was never more than an acquaintance to girls. Although annoying at the time, I later came to appreciate all the "girl problems" God spared me. Little did I know that my time would come.

It was when I walked through the doors as a new student at Bible college that my prospects in marriage took a more promising turn. Before you could spell matrimony, I had a handful of female "friends" who seemed to be just waiting for me to pop the question. These girls lit up like fireflies when I came around, and I liked it! Among the beautiful prospects was an Italian girl, a Singaporean, a girl from Ireland, and a Southern blonde from the good old U.S.A. Praise the Lord for international Bible schools!

Okay guys, in this situation, what does a man after God's own heart do? The most spiritual thing, of course; you pick the prettiest girl. This was my first inclination, but it poses an interesting question: Is the search for a mate no more than a search for the prettiest representative of the opposite sex?

Is the search for a mate no more than a search for the prettiest representative of the opposite sex?

My bliss came to an abrupt end one day when one of these fair daughters of Adam asked me to clarify my intentions in our friendship. On a park bench in the middle of campus, she confided to me that she did care for me, but before our friendship went any further she wanted me to know something. She proceeded to tell me that her life before becoming a believer was less than honorable to God. She did not want to pursue our relationship—and ultimately marriage—any further without me knowing the truth.

This caught me completely off guard, and my brain could not make sense of what my ears were hearing. It wasn't the sin that was so shocking, but rather the direct honesty and courage of this girl in the face of uncertainty. This was truly a girl of virtue, one who was determined to honor God, no matter where the cards fell. Her freedom from her past to walk a righteous life in Christ struck me right between the eyes. Here I was, doing my best to bury my past without ever considering its effect on me and my future bride.

Good problems happen to those who pray.

This girl was no stranger to me. She was a regular participant in an outreach I led to one of the worst parts of Dallas, Texas. By this time, we had worked together for several months in a school evangelism team and, as I was now learning, she was fearless in more ways than one. When she drew a line in the sand of our friendship that day, I began to weigh the merit of all my female friendships. In all of them, I had been upright, except in my love of the game and my delusion that I deserved any of them.

This girl from Ireland, though, was single-handedly ruining everything; is this Murphy's Law or what? After all, couldn't she see? Look at me! Doesn't she realize how lucky she is to have an opportunity at me? Okay, we have chemistry, and she is my best friend, but she knows she isn't the prettiest of my girlfriends, and yet she is willing to put it all on the line for the sake of honesty! And then it

How conceited and vain I was; what I needed was a woman who truly loved and feared the Lord.

hit me, **"Favour is deceitful, and beauty is vain: but a woman that feareth the LORD, she shall be praised."** Proverbs 31:30 Who did I think I was, anyway? I had been looking at this the wrong way all along. How conceited and vain I was; what I needed was a woman who truly loved and feared the Lord.

170

After coming to God's senses, I came to see that this girl had a quality and a strength that set her apart from any other. What she lacked in today's modern definition of glamour and beauty, she made up for in her raw attractiveness and substance. In my experience, the challenge in finding God's choice of a mate lies mainly in one's ability to love what God loves and hate what he hates.

> *The challenge in finding God's choice of a mate lies mainly in one's ability to love what God loves and hate what he hates.*

This perspective will ultimately determine the quality of your choice and your future together. It has never ceased to amaze me how God saved me from myself during this critical decision-making time in my life. If there was anyone who deserved to be in a dead-end, selfish marriage, it was me.

Shortly after this unforgettable conversation on the bench, I, too, confessed to this girl of my ungodly past. What happened next set into motion something completely unexpected and undesired: a realization of my need to confess to people I had defrauded and lied to for years. With her encouragement this was accomplished, and thus a fundamental element for a perfect relationship was established—truth. From that point, we established that there would never be any secrets between us to undermine any future together. During those humiliating days, I was unaware that God was securing for me a future relationship of unspeakable joy, and laying the bedrock for my future understanding of the true gospel of Christ.

> *No choice has paid more dividends than the wife I allowed God to choose for me.*

"God is a Spirit: and they that worship him must worship him in spirit and in truth." John 4:24

In 2012, we will be celebrating twenty-one years of a very happy marriage, and she is still surprising me with her honesty and her love of Jesus. She is the heart and soul of our family, and she still possesses what it takes to have me completely mesmerized by her body and her love. Apart from my new life in Christ, there is nothing I am prouder of or that brings me greater joy than my relationship with my wife. Over the years as I have reflected upon my choices in life, both bad and good, no choice has paid more dividends than the wife I allowed God to choose for me.

My encouragement to you men who are looking for God's choice is to not look. My selfish, active search only brought confusion and anxiety by seeking God to fulfill my bridal wish list. Instead, wrap your whole life around knowing God and fulfilling His commission, and one day you may look around and notice that one of the best helpers in your work could be God's helper for you!

Your Team

You are going to need a help meet who helps you in your life's work. That doesn't mean that if you are a roofer she has to carry shingles up the ladder, or climb under the house if you are a plumber. But she must be fully supportive of your vocation.

You are going to need a help meet who helps you in your life's work.

In the story we just read you will note that Jerry and his bride-to-be were on the same page in their love for evangelism and truth. They still are. They had a lot to talk about other than themselves. They shared a dream, a hope beyond the family. That forms the basis for a rich relationship that will bear good fruit.

What would it have been like if God had created a city girl for Adam? Not that there is anything wrong with a city girl, but, remember, Adam was a farmer. A pampered city girl would have sat on her rattan chair doing her nails, despising the animals and the noisy crickets, and demanded her peaches be canned instead of having to climb the tree to pick them.

On the other hand, what if you are a very neat fellow who likes to entertain and mix with "upper crust" folk, but you marry a messy housekeeper who would rather be in the garden and engaged in cooking herbs into tinctures and running a garage sale on weekends? You would be pulling in different directions. I can tell you for certain, love will not fill the void. You need to find a help meet who will help you, not one who will pull in a different direction.

Teamwork builds character and is lovely to watch. A man who hot-dogs it alone becomes repulsive in the public's eyes; same with the lady. It is important to marry someone who is on the same page.

You may be thinking, "Well, if she really loves me she should be willing to give up her ambitions and follow my leading." Tell me, would it be hard for you to give up your world perspective and follow hers? Of course it would. Well, it will be equally difficult for her to become somebody else for your sake. She may do so, but she will always feel unfulfilled and out of place. When she attends a social event and has to listen to the classy ladies chatter, she will be wishing she had a greenhouse full of plants. Knowing you wish she were different will produce self-condemnation and cause her to always feel rejected and unloved.

---

*Teamwork builds character
and is lovely to watch.*

TIME TO CONSIDER:

Proverbs 22 is one of my favorites.
Read it, study it, and put several key
verses to memory. The wisdom found in
those verses can help you become a river of water. Add this to your
notebook as a life study.

One-Gallon Man
You start off in marriage as a one-gallon man. You may grow to be
a river of life or shrink to become a half pint, depending on whether
you live life as a taker or a giver, a consumer or a provider. If you use
up a wife like a candle burning at both ends to furnish yourself with
light, there will come a time when she has no more wax and you will
be in the dark; but if you dedicate your life to providing her with
more wax, she will be the light of your life.

*Through wisdom is an house
builded; and by understanding it is established.*
Proverbs 24:3

The young man who
honors God will be blessed;
the man who doesn't honor
God can expect nothing.

Chapter 13

THE BLESSED MAN

Some young men want God's blessing on their marriage, but they sit around in the evening playing questionable video games or watching racy movies. Some guys are lazy, yet they are hoping that God will send a miracle girl for them to marry. They shouldn't count on it. The guys who view porn should know that the only thing they will get is regret.

God is not a puppet on the other end of the string of hope. The young man who honors God will be blessed; the man who doesn't honor God can expect nothing. The fellow who is actively seeking God, serving God in ministry of some kind, and being a part of what God is doing can expect a sure help from God.

Here is a story from a blessed man. He came from a family of lost dope smokers and didn't hear the gospel until he was seventeen years old, yet once he believed the gospel, he walked in truth and honor. We know him, thus can bear witness that his life is gloriously blessed.

TJ's Anecdotes on the Greatest Hunt of All

Finding a wife? Choosing a wife? Wow! Where do I start? Besides salvation, WHOM YOU MARRY will be the most crucial, DETERMINING choice of life. I know of nothing in the business, military, or religious world that involves such a lifelong, full-time, 24/7 commitment as does marriage. No secular business partnership even comes close. I find myself aghast and amazed at how lightly people take this issue. The Bible says you and your wife will be **"heirs together of the grace of life."** Much of your career, the spirit of your home, half or more of your social interaction, half or more of your family/in-law affairs, and most of your children's outlook and attitude will be determined by your life mate. The fact that your wife will largely control your finances and will greatly influence your wealth should shake up many of you.

Besides salvation, whom you marry will be the most crucial, determining choice of life.

But most guys will still refuse to hearken to sound counsel. And the whole system is working against you. Your teenage years and early twenties mark the time in life most devoid of wisdom, driven by the strongest passions, when the girls are the sweetest and best looking. Good luck!

It's rough, man! I feel for you guys, and I'm cheering for you. And I can't begin to imagine what it must be like to be a hopeful young lady. If choosing a life mate is scary for a guy, it must be horrifying for the gals. After all, they don't have the same ability to choose whom they will pursue as do we guys. I am SO THANKFUL for the wife God gave me and the relaxed marriage we enjoy. Sometimes I

If choosing a life mate is scary for a guy, it must be horrifying for the gals.

find myself wishing our four children would hurry up, grow up, and move out so that I may have her all to myself once again.

It usually goes without saying that you should know somebody reasonably well before considering them as a spouse. It is also often stated that you will not, indeed cannot, know them real well until AFTER you have been married for some time. Fair enough. What I would have you consider, however, is that knowing YOURSELF can be just as important. Let's back up a little bit and I'll explain why.

First of all, remember that God created man to have dominion over the works of His hands, and has crowned him with glory and honor. Adam was busy fulfilling God's commission when the Lord noted his need for a helper. I know this may not be the most romantic or popular view. Young man, if you have no idea what the purpose for your short time on Planet Earth is, then you might have difficulty choosing an appropriate helper. Instead of toiling and sweating, trying to figure out what kind of a girl to look for, you should make your number-one priority knowing why God has saved you and what he has saved you for. You need details and specifics. It may take months and years, with much prayer and fasting as you seek God's perfect will for your life. It wasn't easy for me, but it sure has paid off. **"But seek ye FIRST the kingdom of God, and his righteousness; and all these things shall be added unto you."** Matthew 6:33 And guys, you

If your current world consists of little more than video games and dreaming of sports cars, then the thought of you being able to wisely choose a suitable helper is humorous at best, and a tragic joke at worst.

can relax; seeking God's will for your life will more than likely NOT result in being sent to the foreign mission field. But if your current world consists of little more than video games and dreaming of sports cars, then the thought of you being able to wisely choose a suitable helper is humorous at best, and a tragic joke at worst.

When I married Kham, I was thirty years old. I had actually been looking at and considering dozens (maybe hundreds?) of girls for nearly twelve years. Man, I'm glad those days are behind me! Hilarious! The point I want to make is that wife hunting wasn't the only thing I had been doing. Far from it.

In fact, a chronology of my life looks like this:

18 yrs. old: Born again in the Lord Jesus Christ
18–20: Extensive study of God's Word,
while working in construction
20: Definite moving of God toward foreign mission with
no idea what or where
20–24: Full-time, specialized training in Bible and missions
25: Led of God to a specific Asian country with no idea what for
25–27: Full-time study of that Asian language
27: Led of the Spirit into Bible translation
30 yrs. old: Married to Kham, who then becomes my chief
helper, secretary, general manager, and cultural broker.

I have an awesome wife. She fits me like a glove. I can barely remember what life was like before her. It's hard to fathom only being together for ten years. She is my favorite object to show off. **"A virtuous woman is a crown to her husband."** Proverbs 12:4 Amen. Get with the program, guys. Find out what your purpose and passion in life is and marry accordingly.

Prepare thy work without,
and make it fit for thyself
in the field; and afterwards
build thine house.
Proverbs 24:27

TIME TO CONSIDER:

How to Become a BLESSED Man:

Psalm 1

Here is a condensed blueprint for success in life that includes three negatives and two positives. Sound simple? It is.

First NO

Blessed is the man that walketh not in the counsel of the ungodly...

Walketh indicates you are just traveling through. Not spending a lot of time but just walking with that person for a short time in your life.

Who are the *ungodly*? Anyone who does not honor God or believe his Word.

What is *counsel*? Receiving advice on any matter such as how to make money, rebuild your marriage, raise your children, or heal your spirit.

Counselors influence people in how they think, what they do, and how they live. People believe they are in control of their own spirits, but this is an illusion. Everything that touches your mind influences you and directs your thought patterns. Movies, video games, books, teachers, and even the news are all molding the way we think about life. Our daily communications have become constant counselors, shaping us and stealing away our future joys.

In his book *Misunderstanding Mental Problems*, Dr. Timothy Scott Rampey demonstrates how gullible people really are. He says, "We have long known that most people readily accept the results of psychological tests—even bogus psychological tests. And we know that when psychological test results are shared, even though the results are bogus, the lives of those receiving that feedback can be dramatically impacted."

For example, it is more effective to give naval officer cadets a phony psychological test evaluation indicating they can quickly overcome seasickness and will perform well at sea than to give them "the pill, patches, and suppositories physicians prescribe."

You are a product of what you allow to pass through your mind.

Second NO

> **Blessed is the man that**
> **walketh not in the counsel of the ungodly,**
> **nor standeth in the way of sinners...**

Standeth indicates hanging-out, finding like-mindedness, and sharing common interests with those who don't love and honor God.

Proverbs is all about the company we maintain. A man decides his fate and chooses his course. He is the captain of his soul and often the destroyer of his family, even before he has a family. Destruction comes from early choices—choices like casually standing in the way of sinners.

Third NO

> **Blessed is the man that walketh not in the**
> **counsel of the ungodly, nor standeth in the way of sinners,**
> **nor sitteth in the seat of the scornful.**

A seated man has arrived. *Scorning* is finding entertainment at the expense of another. Whisperers and backbiters are scornful.

Three things you can't do and be blessed of God: receive counsel from the ungodly, hang out with sinners, and scorn people.

Two Positive Things that Bring God's Blessing

> **But his delight is in the law of the LORD;**
> **and in his law doeth he meditate day and night.**

A blessed man enjoys God's written WORD. He reads and learns the Bible stories. The Word of God is quick, powerful, and effectual; it changes a man's soul; it fills his mind. And what are the natural results of such a thought life?

> **And he shall be like a tree**
> **planted by the rivers of water,**
> **that bringeth forth his fruit in his season;**
> **his leaf also shall not wither;**
> **and whatever he doeth shall prosper.**

God paints a wonderful picture of a good life: a tree that is planted in fertile ground with lots of water and sunshine. You don't have to be concerned with drought or blight. As the years pass you will see such amazing fruit. There will be no heartbreaking stories of your fruit rotting on the tree. You will reap more goodness than you sow.

And then God adds an amazing promise: **"and whatsoever he doeth shall prosper."**

God wants to bless you. He has so many good things he wants to shower on us, if only we avoid these three things and keep our mind on his Word.

What Happens to the Other Crowd?

> **The ungodly are not so:**
> **but are like the chaff which the wind driveth away.**
> **Therefore the ungodly shall not stand in the judgment,**
> **nor sinners in the congregation of the righteous.**

And again God reminds us, **"For the LORD knoweth the way of the righteous: but the way of the ungodly shall perish."**

Three things—only three—that God says NO to.

Two things that God says YES to.

You choose. God delivers.

---

*"A virtuous woman is a
crown to her husband."*
Proverbs 12:4

---

*There are twelve mysteries
in God's Word, but only
the seventh is listed as the
"great mystery."*

Chapter 14

No Greater Love

Jesus is seeking a bride. **"This is a great mystery: but I speak concerning Christ and the church. Nevertheless let every one of you in particular so love his wife even as himself; ..."** Ephesians 5:32-33

There are twelve mysteries in God's Word, but only the seventh is listed as the "great mystery." Each mystery is a strange, beautiful truth that is hard for us to understand. But the greatest of all mysteries is the thought that Jesus has chosen us—fallen humanity—to love and cherish as his bride.

Just as you search for a bride, Jesus is looking for one true, loving friend. He wants a companion with whom to discuss ideas and wonders. He wants a buddy; he designed that our marriages should be a picture and fulfillment of his coming marriage. The mystery is that he has created in man and woman a working, scale model of his relationship to the church throughout eternity. He highly values marriage. Marriage is the closest example of Christ's relationship to his bride, the church. As the man, you are the representative of Christ, loving, caring, giving, healing, and acting as the savior of the body.

Jesus is seeking a bride.

It is indeed a mystery that he chose us, gave his life for us, and will have us to himself for all eternity. It is an honor to God for a man and wife to rejoice, play, laugh, talk, create, work together, and achieve as a couple.

As Christ's bride we come to him full of spots, wrinkles, and blemishes; yet he takes us unto himself with healing and forgiveness—an example of how we are to love our wives **"even as Christ also loved the church, and gave himself for it."** Ephesians 5:25

Ephesians 5:21–33

Submitting yourselves one to another in the fear of God. Wives, submit yourselves unto your own husbands, as unto the Lord. For the husband is the head of the wife, even as Christ is the head of the church: and he is the saviour of the body. Therefore as the church is subject unto Christ, so let the wives be to their own husbands in every thing. Husbands, love your wives, even as Christ also loved the church, and gave himself for it; That he might sanctify and cleanse it with the washing of water by the word, That he might present it to himself a glorious church, not having spot, or wrinkle, or any such thing; but that it should be holy and without blemish. So ought men to love their wives as their own bodies. He that loveth his wife loveth himself. For no man ever yet hated his own flesh; but nourisheth and cherisheth it, even as the Lord the church: For we are members of his body, of his flesh, and of his bones. For this cause shall a man leave his father and mother, and shall be joined unto his wife, and they two shall be one flesh. This is a great mystery: but I speak concerning Christ and the church. Nevertheless let every one of you in particular so love his wife even as himself; and the wife see that she reverence her husband.

No Perfect Girls; Only Perfect Brides

You may be waiting for a match made in heaven. That's good, but remember that heaven is full of grace, tolerance, patience, and a willingness to work with the broken and rejected. You may be just the young man to bring healing to a wounded girl. It is a ministry worthy of divine ordination, and you must be up to the task.

Some men are healers, Priestly in nature. They have very caring hearts. The church will one day be the bride of Christ. The story of Jesus laying down his life for us is all about grace, forgiveness, mercy, and healing. He lifts us up to be his spotless, glorious bride. There are some wonderful young women waiting for their earthly saviors to come and love them, take them by the hand, and make them glorious brides. You may be the man God raises up to bring healing to one of God's most precious girls.

Bringing healing is a ministry worthy of divine ordination.

Most every girl comes to marriage with spots and wrinkles. As the man, it is your job to present your bride to yourself as glorious. In other words, in order to end up with a perfect wife, you start with one that has spots and blemishes and you take the time to sanctify her with love and grace until she becomes the perfect bride; you present her to yourself. A glorious marriage is composed of about 10% of what you start with and 90% of what you make of it through healing, forgiving love.

As you read the next story, reflect on the passage you just read in Psalms 1. This man loves the Word and he is blessed.

Darlin' Bride

I didn't start out to wash my wife with the water of the Word, but if I'd thought about it ahead of time I would have made plans to do just that. As a young man who loved preaching and teaching the Scriptures, everyone in my sphere of influence was my target audience. However, the challenge when I initially met my wife was huge. While teaching Bible doctrine seemed natural, at the moment I met her I was frustrated by my inability to remember my name.

Fortunately, I knew right where to go. Through the fog of her overwhelming beauty I vaguely remembered I'd written my name and address in the front of my Bible in case I were ever separated from it. Turning there quickly, I blurted "Al! "My name is Al! Al is my name!"

I viewed the Word of God as my protector.

At this point she may have thought she was being scolded, and my subsequent resemblance to Pavlov's dog (mouth open and drooling on myself) being somewhat problematic, I did what any young preacher would do. I said, "Got'cher Bible? Turn with me to 1 Corinthians 11…" And so it began.

I viewed the Word of God as my protector. I knew that if I obeyed it, God Almighty himself would honor his Word and protect me. And I realized that I owed it to the person with me to protect her as well as myself. So before there was an us, I took every opportunity to protect myself and her from the enemy's advances by having my Bible with me wherever we went (sitting between us in the truck) and open whenever we weren't traveling. If I wasn't preaching it to others in a public setting, I had it open on the table where we were eating.

I began to observe the changes brought about in her life.

Open in our Christian friends' living rooms. Open on the street when witnessing to lost sinners. Open in the restaurant to teach her and to witness to the waitress. And I was elated to teach someone who was overjoyed to learn what God said about every significant issue in her life. I taught my wife the Scriptures initially for safety's sake more than any reason.

As time passed and my interest in her increased, I began to observe the changes brought about in her life. I knew she'd be going back to college for her senior year following the summer we met, and I challenged her to read the Scriptures daily and to seek God with her whole heart. Never having gone to college a day in my life at that point, I had no idea what I'd tasked her to accomplish. She went back to college and I went back to my Navy base. We began writing letters. Long letters. I'd preach my guts out on legal paper and she'd write back asking questions. I'd study, answer the questions, and preach some more. Her questions often revolved around the structure of the home. I wasn't smart enough to understand the reasons for her questions at the time, but I was a preacher, and I had something to preach (even on paper) so I let'r fly!

I had come from a broken home, but I knew I wasn't going to have one.

I had come from a broken home, but I knew I wasn't going to have one. I grew up in a family of drunkards, but I knew I wasn't going to raise one. I believed what the Scriptures said about training my children, and I told her. I promised her that God's promises were true. I told her she could trust God with every aspect of her life. I had no idea then how much we would one day look back on those promises we found in the Word of God and the comfort and safety we would experience. Without understanding what I was doing, my investment in a sister was an investment in our home. After we married and some of her relatives wanted her to leave me because we were broke, she trusted God with me. When both of our families wanted to have our children taken from us for our training methods, we ran from our families, and she trusted God with me. We learned

The hallmark of our home has been—what does God say about it?

to trust God individually before we were a couple. We learned to trust by reading and believing his Word. I didn't know what else to teach but to trust what he said. And this has been a hallmark in our home—what does God say about it?

As time passed I began to consider whether or not this woman might be my wife from the Lord. I also realized that my preaching would take me to foreign countries. And I would need a wife to assist

My encouragement to her became the clear direction of my life.

me in these endeavors. To me that meant high adventure. To a potential wife that usually means bugs. And wild animals. This woman was not uninterested. She was terrified! And I knew that my wife was going to have to be willing to go anywhere God told me to go with a smile on her face and thankfulness in her heart. In military jargon, she had to be "all in." Since she wasn't, I immediately decided in my heart "She's NOT the ONE!" (Patience may be a virtue, but it was never my strong suit!) I was interested in finding my wife, but I wasn't interested in having a girlfriend. Those who knew me were aware of my position. I told the woman I would eventually marry that I

"Mike, you reckon God has a sense of humor?" Without looking up or slowing down, he answered, "Of course he does, stupid. He made you, didn't he?"

was going to get out of the military and I was going to follow the Lord. I had no other option. Before I left I counseled her that even though she was a brand-new college graduate, she should not trust in her education but embrace God's promises for her provision. I told her that she could be sure that God would provide for her if she would trust him. My encouragement to her became the clear direction of my life.

I left the military with full intention of working, saving money, and going to the jungle. My desire was truly to be God's missionary. I thought that was God's plan. It was not—not in the jungle anyway. When I left her behind, I extracted promises from my family and friends that if this young woman asked for my contact information, they were not to provide it. I was going to the jungle and was not to be encumbered by anything. Young men have so much to learn! I learned that God is not only longsuffering with young men, but that he has a sense of humor as well.

This was illustrated to me one day while working in the barn. A wise preacher (who has always looked much older than he is and appears even wiser because of it) and I were busy making craft products to sell in the local mall during the holiday season. Suddenly struck by the thought, I asked, "Mike, you reckon God has a sense of humor?" Without looking up or slowing down, he answered, "Of course he does, stupid. He made you, didn't he?" While Mike stood there laughing, I went for a walk to get my face back to its normal color. I walked slowly down to the mailbox to recover and to see if maybe I had received a letter. (This was back in the old days when people used things like paper, pens, envelopes, and stamps.) I didn't know who I'd get a letter from, but I went looking anyway. Divine providence indeed!

I told her she could trust God with every aspect of her life. I had no idea then how much we would one day look back on those promises we found in the Word of God and the comfort and safety we would experience.

When I got there, I saw a letter addressed to me and grew excited. From my hometown! From who? What? My friends and family had honored their commitment not to provide my contact information if asked. They didn't wait to be asked. They called her! She had more questions and didn't trust the folks around her with their commercial Bibles to provide truth. She wanted more answers. So I answered her questions. And my answers always began with, "Sister, God bless you for your desire to know him more fully." I didn't know if I'd marry this woman or not, but I knew that I was going to answer to God for what I said and how I said it. And if she were to be my wife, I wasn't going to wait for someone else to teach her.

Well, she closed in for the kill. She started writing about how God had dealt with her about how she could honor God by honoring her husband. She wrote about having and raising babies. How she had prayed those children would grow up to bring honor to the God who had saved her. Well, I guess my turkey was fried by that point. I wrote back to her. I began as always, "Sister, God bless you…" and this time I finished with "…for desiring his best for your life."

> *I began as always "Sister, God bless you…" and this time I finished with "…for desiring his best for your life."*

I prayed for several weeks for God to give me a sign if she were the one. Some may think this spiritually immature and perhaps it was, but God answered my prayer in a dream that was crystal clear. In the dream I was standing with my bride alongside me, and a voice said, "This is what you've been waiting for." I awoke immediately, got out of bed and on my knees and thanked God profusely. We were married just a few months later.

My ministry has taken me everywhere but the jungle. I returned to my beloved Navy and served God there for twenty-two years. I've drawn crosses in the sand on the beaches in Okinawa and witnessed to little Japanese boys. I've handed out gospel tracks in Muslim countries by myself when I couldn't get others to go with me. I've preached

> *God is a faithful fellow indeed and his Word is true.*

onboard ship and in port. And I've witnessed and testified to the most senior officers in the military. Without my faithful, praying wife back home, I'd have accomplished much less. She was back home praying for me and believing what I'd taught her years before—that if we trusted God, he would protect and provide. He's a faithful fellow indeed and his Word is true.

The Darlin' Bride and I married a little over 28 years ago. It's flown by. Yesterday we were thinking about having kids, and today we have five wonderful young adult children who bring us great joy and pride, and two splendid grandsons that I call The Sons of Thunder.

Before I met my wife I wanted our home to be founded and focused on the Word of God. When I met her I taught her the Word of God for her sake, for my sake, and for God's sake. Over these last many years, my wife has often told the story that she chose me because she knew from hearing me teach her the Scriptures that I was going to honor the Lord. She claims that my testimony was consistent with what she heard.

While many of my contemporaries might have preferred to be chosen because they were tall, dark, and handsome, I was not afflicted with any of those maladies! And while the Darlin' Bride is incomparably beautiful, she, like me, wanted a home that was built upon the safety of the Word of God and not on fleeting beauty. God gave us the desires of our hearts and we continue to trust his Word for our lives. I am truly a blessed man.

NOTE: The author of this story is the man who wrote the seven lessons at the back of the book. We think he was right on in teaching his prospective bride, so we asked him to pass on his experience in a form that will allow others to duplicate his road to wisdom.

When I met my wife I taught her the Word of God for her sake, for my sake, and for God's sake.

TIME TO CONSIDER:

Charity: 1 Corinthians 13

Charity is a working form of true love. It is the acting out of love.

Charity begins at home. If you don't have charity toward your wife then you are nothing. God uses an entire chapter to describe what love is. Open your Bible and read 1 Corinthians chapter 13.

The first three verses tell us what charity is **not**. It is not being so spiritual that you can speak in tongues; it is not having a gift of prophecy or having great faith. Charity is not the act of giving your money or even sacrificing your life for another.

> **Charity suffereth long, and is kind;**
> **charity envieth not;**
> **charity vaunteth not itself, is not puffed up,**
> **Doth not behave itself unseemly, seeketh not her own,**
> **is not easily provoked,**
>
> **Charity thinketh no evil;**
> **Rejoiceth not in iniquity, but rejoiceth in the truth;**
> **Beareth all things,**
> **believeth all things,**
> **hopeth all things,**
> **endureth all things.**
> **Charity never faileth.**

Notice one sign of charity and maturity is found in verse 11: **"When I was a child, I spake as a child, I understood as a child, I thought as a child: but when I became a man, I put away childish things."**

As a man of God, one sign of true maturity and charity is putting away time-wasting childish things.

Verse 12 tells us, **"For now we see through a glass darkly; but then face to face: now I know in part; but then shall I know even as also I am known."** As men we walk by faith, honoring God and loving our lady even when she seems not so sweet and kind; we have made a commitment to love and continue to love regardless of the circumstance. **"Charity never faileth."**

The conclusion of chapter 13 reminds us that although we may think we have succeeded in life, as a preacher, teacher, provider, and friend to all, if we have not shown charity to that one person closest to us, then all is in vain. **"And now abideth faith, hope, charity, these three; but the greatest of these is charity."**

Charity never faileth.
1 Corinthians 13:8

Iron sharpeneth iron;
so a man sharpeneth
the countenance of his friend.
Proverbs 27:17

Chapter 15

THAT I MAY BE LIKE HIM

**For all the law is fulfilled in one word, even in this;
Thou shalt love thy neighbour as thyself.** ^{Galatians 5:14}

Our purpose on this earth is to develop character—to love and
sacrifice for the benefit of others, especially those in our care. Only in
developing character and virtue do we realize God's purposes for us
humans. It is a well-worn and true statement that we fight against the
world, the flesh, and the devil. Many married men end up thinking
their struggle is against the world, the flesh, the devil, and the wife.
The most devastating enemy is not any of these; it is our own selfish
mind.

As I discussed at length in
my book *By Divine Design*, there
are some things God cannot do.
He cannot create character, but
the world, the flesh, the devil,
and, yes, a wife can. Character
comes as we make right choices
in the face of conflicting values

*Character comes as we make
right choices in the face of
conflicting values and the
temptation to seek our own
to the exclusion of others.*

and the temptation to seek our own to the exclusion of others.
Marriage will provide the conflict as two people compete for the
same space. Two life perspectives vie for survival. Marriage is God's
character clinic because there is no environment that so tests one's
patience as the family. There are many men who appear beautiful on

the outside, but within they are full of rudeness, pride, anger, and bitterness. What you hide in public you release at home. Being with a person every day, week after week, and year after year will reveal one's true heart. So we might say that marriage is an obstacle course for the heart. All of us bring to marriage a pretty good load of pride, selfishness, stubbornness, and self-will. Your relationship to your wife will either enable you to overcome your carnal ways or kick you over the edge into the world of pride and hypocrisy.

Marriage is an obstacle course for the heart.

You need a woman who will make the battle easier, not one who battles you for supremacy. The right woman—or might I say, a woman who is right—will make it much easier for you to grow within rather than rot within.

Marriage presses two people into a tight relationship where they can no longer hide who they are. Your parents think they know you, but they don't. You won't even know yourself until you have a wife to test your patience and try your limitations. Life is a character clinic, and marriage is the headquarters. Marriage can be either ground zero, where you grind one another into powder, or it can be a heavenly pinnacle where you sanctify each other to become worthy sons and daughters of God. As **"iron sharpeneth iron"** by the process of two hard surfaces rubbing against each other, husband and wife will sharpen each other or else they will create enough heat to generate a meltdown. With time, marriages either improve or implode. A couple learns to soar together or they sour separately. You learn to give everything, or everything that is precious is taken away from you.

You won't even know yourself until you have a wife to test your patience and try your limitations.

You will either put yourself under or the two of you will put your marriage asunder. Your souls must merge as do your bodies. The old identity is lost and the new "y'all" is born. When sand and cement are mixed, you no longer have sand and you no longer have cement, but you have something much stronger—concrete. If sand wants to cling to its identity, it will be carried away in the wind and remembered no more. But if it humbles itself to become a blend, it will last well beyond a lifetime.

A couple learns to soar together or they sour separately.

Adam failed his very first test by making the wrong choice, choosing to investigate the dark side. So he fell out of God's good graces, plunging the human race into his history of bad choices, causing each of us to be born out of touch with our Creator and possessed of a soul disconnected from our only source of positive development.

In time God sent his Son to the earth in human form so he could take the character test that Adam and all his descendents had failed. Jesus lived thirty-three years in perfect harmony with God's

Your souls must merge as do your bodies. The old identity is lost and the new "y'all" is born.

law and qualified to be a representative of the human race before the bar of God. His first act as righteous man was to die the death we all deserve and then overcome death through his resurrection. The overcoming man now sits on the right hand of the Father representing mankind and interceding on our behalf.

Upon his return to heaven, Jesus sent the very Spirit of God to indwell those who would choose God over their own pleasures and glory. Those who are indwelt by that Spirit are now enrolled in God's character class and are daily becoming more of what our Creator intended for us to become when he first began the human journey.

Paul correctly observed, **But he that is married careth for the things that are of the world, how he may please his wife.** 1 Corinthians 7:33

It is God's will for you to care to please your wife. When you are married, you have no right to care for other things first, not even ministry. If you are a preacher or missionary, your first calling is to your wife and children, not your ministry. Ministry begins at home, and one is even disqualified from the ministry if his home is not in order. 1 Timothy 3:4

The union of man and woman in marriage is the process of two becoming one: **"…so then they are no more twain, but one flesh. What therefore God hath joined together, let not man put asunder."** Mark 10:8, 9

It is no wonder that God calls this glorious union of man and maid a mystery—a great mystery!

---

*God wants you to grow
in character and fulfill
his original intention
for the human race.*

TIME TO CONSIDER:

Make an outline of this passage as if it will be a speech or sermon.

Philippians 3:13–21

Brethren, I count not myself to have apprehended: but this one thing I do, forgetting those things which are behind, and reaching forth unto those things which are before, I press toward the mark for the prize of the high calling of God in Christ Jesus.

Let us therefore, as many as be perfect, be thus minded: and if in any thing ye be otherwise minded, God shall reveal even this unto you. Nevertheless, whereto we have already attained, let us walk by the same rule, let us mind the same thing.

Brethren, be followers together of me, and mark them which walk so as ye have us for an ensample. (For many walk, of whom I have told you often, and now tell you even weeping, that they are the enemies of the cross of Christ: Whose end is destruction, whose God is their belly, and whose glory is in their shame, who mind earthly things.)

For our conversation is in heaven; from whence also we look for the Saviour, the Lord Jesus Christ: Who shall change our vile body, that it may be fashioned like unto his glorious body, according to the working whereby he is able even to subdue all things unto himself.

*A virtuous woman is a crown to
her husband: but she that maketh
ashamed is as rottenness in his bones.*

Proverbs 12:4

Chapter 16

UNIVERSAL WONDER-WIFE

You are searching for the perfect help meet? The Bible describes her very well. She is the universal wonder-wife. We cannot do better than using Proverbs 31 as our guide. It describes in detail the virtues of a most excellent wife. Verse 1 tells us King Lemuel recorded the prophecy that his mother taught him.

Then she begins a quick outline of Proverbs. In verse 3 she reminds him that women have destroyed kings; not just regular dudes, but kings as well.

In verses 4 and 5 she reminds him that strong drink (alcohol) will cause him to forget the law and pervert good judgment.

In verses 6 and 7 she tells her son where there is a worthy use of alcohol— for those who are ready to perish or those whose lives are so miserable all they can do is forget who and what they are. It is not for a man who has a future.

These are the things that a man of judgment and leadership has to follow or he will surely bring many to ruin.

In verse 8 she reminds him to remember those who cannot speak for themselves; to be kind.

In verse 9 she tells him to always speak up for righteous judgment. It is not enough to be a good man; you must speak up for those who might be mistreated, needy, or poor.

These are the things that a man of judgment and leadership must follow or he will surely bring many to ruin. Then she remembers that unless her son, a coming king, can find a worthy wife who will help him walk in these steps and cause him to be free to serve others, all is still lost. She gives him a picture of a universal wonder woman so he will know her when he meets her. Mama Lemuel starts off by saying, **"Who can find a virtuous woman? For her price is far above rubies."**

The Virtuous Woman

As you read Proverbs 31, think about choosing a wife with these qualities.

10 Who can find a virtuous woman? for her price is far above rubies.

11 The heart of her husband doth safely trust in her, so that he shall have no need of spoil.

12 She will do him good and not evil all the days of her life.

13 She seeketh wool, and flax, and worketh willingly with her hands.

14 She is like the merchants' ships; she bringeth her food from afar.

15 She riseth also while it is yet night, and giveth meat to her household, and a portion to her maidens.

16 She considereth a field, and buyeth it: with the fruit of her hands she planteth a vineyard.

17 She girdeth her loins with strength, and strengtheneth her arms.

18 She perceiveth that her merchandise is good: her candle goeth not out by night.

19 She layeth her hands to the spindle, and her hands hold the distaff.

20 She stretcheth out her hand to the poor; yea, she reacheth forth her hands to the needy.

21 She is not afraid of the snow for her household: for all her household are clothed with scarlet.

22 She maketh herself coverings of tapestry; her clothing is silk and purple.

23 Her husband is known in the gates, when he sitteth among the elders of the land.

24 She maketh fine linen, and selleth it; and delivereth girdles unto the merchant.

25 Strength and honour are her clothing; and she shall rejoice in time to come.

26 She openeth her mouth with wisdom; and in her tongue is the law of kindness.

27 She looketh well to the ways of her household, and eateth not the bread of idleness.

28 Her children arise up, and call her blessed; her husband also, and he praiseth her.

29 Many daughters have done virtuously, but thou excellest them all.

30 Favour is deceitful, and beauty is vain: but a woman that feareth the LORD, she shall be praised.

31 Give her of the fruit of her hands; and let her own works praise her in the gates.

To be holy in character AND wholly valuable as a helper is the ultimate virtuous woman.

What is virtue? It is first moral purity, but the biblical definition as seen in its eleven usages is broader than just moral purity—as is the case in common usage. It also speaks of that which is highly valued for its excellent qualities. The Proverbs 31 woman is pure and moral, but she is so much more than that. A woman could have moral virtue without being worth much as a wife or person. To be holy in character AND wholly valuable as a helper is the ultimate virtuous woman.

Proverbs 31:10-31 Verse By Verse

10 Who can find a virtuous woman? for her price is far above rubies.

The passage begins with the issue at hand—the difficulty of finding a virtuous woman.

"Who can find" indicates a lot of men have been looking with a great deal of disappointment and frustration. It seems superfluous to state the obvious, but my audience is broad. Settle in your heart; are you indeed looking for a virtuous woman? Many guys aren't. They are admiring any number of qualities, but they have not placed absolute moral purity at the top of their list.

What kind of girls attract you today? Are you stimulated by gals who are slack in their moral convictions? If so, then the difficulty of finding a virtuous woman has not been a major concern to you. If you flirt with folly, you will fall for folly and fail in a fool's paradise.

"…for her price is far above rubies." Three times the Bible tells us that the price of wisdom is above rubies. Job 28:18; Proverbs 3:13-15; Proverbs 8:11 And here we read that the price of a virtuous woman is **"far"** above rubies. If we value what God values, we will search diligently for a woman of supreme virtue and look with pity upon those pretty twits who tweet their shame and advertise their wantonness rather than their wisdom.

I'm reminded of a story I heard through our ministry of a young man who was seeking a bride. Through a friend he heard about this really beautiful, godly girl. His parents had mentioned her name several times, obviously dropping a hint, so he decided to call a few of his friends who knew her and ask their opinion of her. They all agreed that she was a godly girl who would match him very well. This sounded promising. He drove several hours one Sunday morning to visit her church. The girl was a smashing beauty—much more beautiful than anyone had even said. After church he introduced himself to her family as a friend of so-and-so, which resulted in an invitation to family dinner. All was going as planned. Her big dark eyes and flashing smile wowed him all afternoon, and he left feeling tingly with anticipation. How good can it get?

A friend of his had told him to always check out a girl on Facebook and Twitter before going forward with anything because it reveals much about a girl. He had never done the social network thing, but he decided to use his friend's sister's account to check out this beautiful gal. What she wrote wasn't evil and the pictures she posted weren't too vain, but her overall life was an empty jangle. No

Her virtue will provide sign posts and rest stops for the weary pilgrim.

mention of any type of ministry, prayer, concern for politics, health, or even fitness. Every day was filled with a lot of nonsense. She also had a habit of ridiculing others. Her conversation lacked virtue. He visited her again, hoping to regain the brightness, but now he heard a side of her that he hadn't noticed before. She was history.

Another girl, not nearly so pretty or talented or even highly recommended, came to his attention a short time later. Put through even closer scrutiny, he discovered that this gal had substance and virtue. She was mama material. Today she is a mighty fine mama to his growing number of kids. Most young men are devoid of wisdom and a wise perspective. I would that young men could only see how highly valuable is a woman of great virtue. There will come a time in marriage that little else matters. Her virtue will be a frame of reference that keeps you stable when walking in a world of moral quicksand. Her virtue will provide sign posts and rest stops for the weary pilgrim. She will be the bridge over troubled waters, whereas a woman of low virtue will be a weight around the neck of a man trying to tread water in a deep ocean.

> **Be ye not unequally yoked together with unbelievers: for what fellowship hath righteousness with unrighteousness? and what communion hath light with darkness?** 2 Corinthians 6:14

11 The heart of her husband doth safely trust in her, so that he shall have no need of spoil.

The husband trusts that his wife will not place a financial burden upon him. (see verses 12–19). Therein is her first virtue.

Her first virtue is her diligent handling of business matters.

You will see in succeeding texts, because of the wife's financial contribution, the husband has no need to take spoil. Spoil is valuables or property taken by the victor in conflict. The winner of a law suit spoils his opponent. A hostile takeover of a business spoils the assets of the business. A landlord who does not meet his obligations to keep up the property of poor tenants spoils the renters. A thief spoils a home when he breaks and enters. Dishonest salesmen spoil buyers.

How marvelous and liberating it is to the heart of a husband to have a wife who is so frugal and careful in the way she handles the family's resources that he is never tempted to increase his income by spoiling others. He needs not fear that her spending will bring them to poverty.

The heart of her husband trusts in her. That indicates his trust is on a much deeper level than the trust one has in a faithful employee or friend. His spirit is at rest as he safely trusts in her. A virtuous woman assures a man that there is safety in her loyalty to him. His trust is well placed. He will not be ashamed or embarrassed by her.

12 She will do him good and not evil all the days of her life.

This is part of that introductory statement that will be expanded upon in the following description of the virtuous acts of this woman whose value is greater than rubies. Note her virtue is seen in the things she does—she will **"do him good."** The next verse commences with the specifics of what she does that qualify her as a virtuous woman.

Her virtue is in her industriousness

Her virtue is in her industriousness. Look at the first two verses together.

"Who can find a virtuous woman? for her price is far above rubies. The heart of her husband doth safely trust in her, so that he shall have no need of spoil." Proverbs 31:10-11 As is often the case in Scripture, the first sentence of a passage makes a statement that is then expounded upon in the following verses. So it is here. The subject is that a virtuous woman is rare, worth more than expensive rubies because of her contribution to the material welfare of the family. Her monetary worth will exceed the value of expensive rubies. Her virtue is in her industriousness.

Look out now! I, rather King Solomon, has committed an unpardonable infraction against conservative dogma by adding to the book of Proverbs this queen's prophecies given to her son, King Lemuel. The passage is clearly speaking contrary to fundamental orthodoxy by saying that a virtuous woman is an entrepreneur and assists in the family income.

13 She seeketh wool, and flax, and worketh willingly with her hands.
24 She maketh fine linen, and selleth it; and delivereth girdles unto the merchant.

She is a **"keeper at home,"** Titus 2:3 taking care of the children, cleaning house, and preparing meals, but she finds time to seek the best prices on raw wool and flax, which she then spins and weaves Proverbs 31:19 into fine fabric that she sells Proverbs 31:24 at a good profit—her income eventually exceeding the price of rubies.

Obviously, today a woman is not going to take up spinning and weaving unless, of course, she is into craft items that have a value that exceeds their practical usefulness, in which case she might also make candles or soap. The principle thing is that she is industrious and entrepreneurial, seeing a need in the market and filling it.

> *The principle thing is that she is industrious and entrepreneurial, seeing a market and filling it.*

Wow! This is so different from what I was taught coming up. It was a matter of sacred dogma that a woman was not to so much as pay the bills. She was supposed to do nothing but domestic chores and leave all money and business matters to her husband.

The timeless principle is stated last: she **"worketh willingly with her hands."** This is just the first in a long list of virtues, and it already eliminates the vast majority of high-maintenance girls who expect to become prima donnas placed on pedestals and pandered to.

This is not just about the degree of financial contribution she makes to the family; it is a matter of character and self-esteem. There is moral virtue in being a maker and not just a taker. Children take, but they are supposed to grow up to make for the benefit of others.

Additionally, a hard-working woman is more lovely than a lazy one. A woman who is achieving goals and doing things of value will feel better about herself, and for that reason will be a happier person, even if her financial contribution is insignificant.

The first calling and responsibility of a woman with children is to be a **"keeper at home"** and though most of her energies will be dedicated to training the children and keeping the home, she may have some creative energy that must find an outlet. The happiest children are the ones most

> *The happiest children are the ones most engaged in being productive.*

engaged in being productive. If a mother can find a way to involve the children in productive projects, it is a win-win situation all the way around.

If you are checking out an eighteen-year-old girl living at home with six brothers and sisters, it is not likely that she will be engaged in any financially profitable enterprise, but you can tell where her heart is by looking closely at how she spends her extra time. It is a simple matter. Is she working "willingly with her hands"? Does she lead her younger brothers and sisters in creative projects like planting a garden, keeping up the yard, painting the house? Does she help out at public charities or at church? Does she speak of a vision of accomplishing something in life? Is she enthusiastic about the challengers of life?

Marriage is a bicycle built for two. The husband rides up front and controls the steering but there are two sets of pedals, and the whole thing goes faster and is more likely to get where you want to go when both riders are pedaling. Marriage is also like a bicycle built for two in that both riders must lean in the same direction, first one way and then the other, when weaving through the issues of life. Imagine having a wife who leans in the opposite direction. You might lose control of the steering and the marriage would crash.

14 She is like the merchants' ships; she bringeth her food from afar.

She is of great value to her husband, because she is very selective and inventive in providing her family with good food from distant places. This is far more important than you can possibly image unless you have been raised in a family that is very healthy-diet conscious. Healthy eating is the discipline of self-denial. Because some foods are so devoid of nutrients, it is more important than ever to familiarize oneself with the nutrient requirements of the body and what each food provides. If you live in Minnesota it will be necessary to buy citrus fruit **"from afar."** A woman who is willing to use great discretion in the food she provides for her family is worth more than rubies because she will save the family major medical bills and a world of pain. A man will live longer and be much more productive married to a woman who is discerning and creative in her food shopping. If you think it takes more money to eat well, you are uninformed. You will definitely need a woman who can *help meet* your daily nutrient requirements. Pun intended, of course.

There is moral virtue in being a maker and not just a taker.

15 She riseth also while it is yet night, and giveth meat to her household, and a portion to her maidens.

This is just too good to be true for us Southern boys. He is talking about a good old-fashioned country woman. **"She riseth up while it is yet night"** to cook a pan of whole-wheat biscuits made from organically grown grain which she had shipped in from Nebraska and distributed in a co-op, leaving her with enough profit to provide wheat for her family and additional money to buy organic vegetables for a whole year. In addition to the biscuits, she serves organic butter and eggs from free-range chickens and finishes it off with some homemade blackberry jam, which she and the girls canned last summer. Mmm—I am so in love.

I can remember my youth. I had to ride the bus for an hour and a half to get to public school. Every morning I was awakened before daylight to the smell of freshly cooked biscuits and oatmeal or eggs or rice. As soon as I hopped out of bed and pulled on my clothes, I ran to the table to take my fill.

While this mother is increasing the family wealth she is developing the character of her children—a great virtue.

My mother was a virtuous woman. I didn't know it at the time, but after I was grown I came to realize that there were times when we were very poor. Yet my mother never missed preparing a meal. There were plenty of times that we didn't have any meat, but we always had beans and cornbread with a slice of onion and some fresh vegetables during growing season—espccially sliced tomatoes. I love tomatoes to this day. I even eat them for breakfast.

So how is getting up early to prepare a meal of greater value than rubies? Well, she would save approximately $8,000 a year vs. the family eating a fast-food breakfast out, and that for just the breakfast meal alone. That is about the value of two very nice rubies. And the eventual savings in dental and medical bills will amount to a handful of rubies in value. The psychological effect is priceless.

16 She considereth a field, and buyeth it: with the fruit of her hands she planteth a vineyard.

This woman is of virtue to her husband because she carefully analyzes the real estate market and makes a wise choice in the purchase of a piece of idle land, which she then turns into a long-term investment, planting grapes that will in time produce an income.

Apparently she made enough money from the sale of the fabric she spun and wove to purchase the land, so she is reinvesting her profits to seek greater profit. She is a capitalist first-class.

It says **"with the fruit of her hands she planteth a vineyard."** That means she got down and dirty, doing the planting herself. There is nothing better for kids than to be involved in productive projects with their parents. While this mother is increasing the family wealth, she is developing the character of her children—a great virtue.

Again, a young girl will not have had time to become a real estate speculator or the owner of a vineyard, but you should look carefully to see if she has seized upon the opportunities that are available to her. Does she babysit for money? Does she clean houses for profit or as a ministry to someone? Either way, it shows a willingness to work. Has she purchased books on gardening or some other worthy endeavor and then tried her hand at it? Girls don't change when they get married except to become more of what they are. Don't expect love will turn a lazy gal into a hard-working woman.

17 She girdeth her loins with strength, and strengtheneth her arms.

This is so hip. A virtuous woman is a fitness freak. She is not a physical slacker. She takes steps to keep her body strong. Every man is attracted to a physically fit woman. You never see advertisements featuring slouchy women. They are always in top shape because that is what is attractive to men and women alike. The key to being physically fit is that it requires self-denial—a character trait. Slack and pudgy is the default position of those who do not exert any effort. So it is an act of character to stay fit, as it is a lack of character to allow one's self to become the victim of

The key to being physically fit is that it requires self-denial—a character trait.

inactivity or overeating—or indiscreet eating.

There is a problem here since most women are not physically fit, but then most men are not physically fit either. If you are a lazy slouch you may want to marry a lazy slouch so you won't be constantly reminded of your lack of commitment to good health. It would be a real bummer to have a wife who jumps up to exercise while you eat sweet cereal and milk. So if this passage of Scripture doesn't motivate you to want a woman with this level of virtue, at least it will keep you from marrying one who will make you hate yourself every time she comes in sweating from working in the garden.

18 She perceiveth that her merchandise is good: her candle goeth not out by night.
19 She layeth her hands to the spindle, and her hands hold the distaff.

This passage emphasizes her determination and commitment to continue being productive. The spindle and distaff speak of spinning and weaving fabric. Of course today, other than as a craft or hobby, no one in the Western world still spins and weaves

She doesn't wait for life to be handed to her. Diligence *is the word that comes to mind.*

as a matter of practical necessity. But the principle remains the same. This virtuous woman **"perceiveth"** that she has a product that is in high demand in the marketplace, so she works day and night to get it ready for delivery, not wanting to miss the window of opportunity.

Diligence is the word that comes to mind when I read this passage. This woman has a fire in her that drives her to achieve, to strike while the iron is hot. She doesn't wait for life to be handed to her. She makes a judgment about the demands of the marketplace and jumps to fill the need.

Note the statement, **"She layeth her hands to the spindle, and her hands hold the distaff."** She is known for putting her hands to the task at hand. She doesn't just dream; she does it with her own hands. What a gal!

Again, most girls are not going to be busy little bees. Most are dependent and weak, expecting husband to be like Daddy, placing food before them and giving them money to buy clothes. They want to spend their days shopping and talking and taking little trips to the mall. In the evening they are too tired to prepared supper from scratch, so rather than bring their food from afar, they pop prepared, processed, dead foods into the microwave and serve their husbands another dose of early death.

Some people go to the market and sell; others go to buy. Decide which one you are and marry the same.

You may be one of those guys who just doesn't care to make a mark in the world and you don't expect anything else from a wife. If so, then please don't marry one of those firebrands who is ready to stay up all night to bring a new project to fruition. Save her for a guy who wants to conquer and leave his mark on the world, and in the process you will save yourself from a lot of intimidation and self-loathing.

This is good advice you are getting here. I know that not every guy and gal are perfect, contrary to what Mom and Dad think. And birds of a feather need to flock together. Above all, don't try to marry success. She will drag you to death or leave you choking in her dust. At the very least she will keep you awake at night with the sound of her spinning wheel. Some people go to the market and sell; others go to buy. Decide which one you are and marry the same.

**20 She stretcheth out her hand to the poor;
yea, she reacheth forth her hands to the needy.**

This woman is beginning to look like Wonderful Woman indeed. Not only is she in great physical condition, preparing balanced nutritional meals and conducting profitable business on the side, she takes time to do charity work with the poor and needy. She is not working herself to a frazzle just to get ahead financially; she has a heart of compassion for those less fortunate than she. She might observe that the hungry do not work as hard as she does, but, no, she just sees a need and rushes to meet it without judgment.

On a side note, there is a lesson here to be learned about the nature of capitalism. There is not a more compassionate political system than free enterprise. Where one is free to benefit from the fruit of one's labor, that person is more likely to freely give to those less fortunate. I call that trickle-down compassion.

I have observed young girls who twiddled away their time waiting to get married, passing up opportunities to be of service to others, not visiting the old folk, and not engaging themselves in fighting abortion or human slavery, rather just waiting for life to begin with marriage. When these girls get married they are no more useful than they were before marriage. They still live unto themselves. Some mothers hang on to their daughters so tightly, hoping to spare them from the world, that neither mother nor daughter are of any use. They are training their daughters to be NON-virtuous.

A compassionate, productive single girl is a compassionate, productive married girl.

If you are a man of compassion, a man with a Priestly nature who likes to lend a hand or an ear, then you will need to marry a girl with a heart as big as yours or you may discover that you are married to a woman who is jealous of your sharing yourself with others. If you are going to **"weep with those that weep,"** you are going to need a gal who feels for others as you do.

21 She is not afraid of the snow for her household:
for all her household are clothed with scarlet.
22 She maketh herself coverings of tapestry; her clothing
is silk and purple.

It is readily apparent in Scripture that scarlet is always associated with that which is very fine and beautiful. It was the color of wealth and prestige, and silk was an imported rarity. This virtuous woman who spins and weaves her own fabric and sells it in the marketplace is able to clothe her husband and children with the very best and warmest of garments. The clothes were not only practical, they were beautiful as well—very mod.

Her industriousness enables her to dress her family well and so she does. She is mod.

So we can conclude that this woman of great value is no slouch. She doesn't project her spirituality by dressing her family like paupers or poor Amish wanna-bes. Her industriousness enables her to dress her family well and so she does. She does not forget the poor and needy, but neither is she possessed of such guilt that she shuns showing her wealth.

I would not have written this as it is; I rather favor plainness in dress, but then God didn't consult me when he wrote it, so I am confined to the inspired text just as it stands and must respect what it says.

I have always been leery of a girl who wants to dress flamboyantly all the time. Now there is nothing wrong with—in fact, there is something very right about—a young unmarried girl dressing up like a peacock trying to attract a mate. It is the way of nature, I am sure. And it is quite appropriate for an old married lady to dress fit-to-be-bred for a night out with her husband. These things are good and wholesome. But there is a fine line so easy to cross. Dressing sexy and elegant are two totally different things. Sexy says cheap—no virtue; elegant says worth much. But when a woman gets her self-image from never being seen unless properly made up, she has stopped being herself and is projecting a lie. She will not be a happy woman, for she lives in fear of people discovering the real person behind the clothes and make-up.

> **"In like manner also, that women adorn themselves in modest apparel, with shamefacedness and sobriety; not with broided hair, or gold, or pearls, or costly array; But (which becometh women professing godliness) with good works."** 1 Timothy 2:9-10

There are some men who like a pasty-faced, red-lipped lollypop that has no practical use—and the flavor and odor are artificial. If you do, this book will be of no value to you in finding a help meet. It is a pity that God gives a woman one face and she makes herself another.

23 Her husband is known in the gates, when he sitteth among the elders of the land.

Due to her highly visible activity in real estate and manufacturing, her fine appearance in scarlet and silk, and her charity work, this woman has come to the attention of the men of the city so that it raises the esteem of her husband in the eyes of the leaders of the city. In other words, this woman is of virtue in providing her husband with an open door to the influential people of the city. She has not exerted herself to the end of exercising self-promoting influence, but the byproduct of her success is the promotion of her husband. He gets the credit for her deeds.

Strength of spirit is associated with moral courage, knowledge, and wisdom.

I have seen this fruit borne in thousands of cases. It is always assumed that a good woman must be the result of a good man. So he is honored when she is honorable, and he gets the dishonor when she is a lazy slouch.

Again, you may not want to sit in the gate with the influential people. And you may not care to wear a silk shirt produced in your wife's Hong Kong factory, but that is a choice you need to make before you marry a fine girl who is already pointed in some direction. Save the girls who can change the world for the men who want to be a part of eternal events. I urge you to find out which way she is pointed before you get emotionally involved.

25 Strength and honour are her clothing; and she shall rejoice in time to come.

Strength of spirit is what he speaks of in this passage—moral courage. It is associated with knowledge and wisdom in many other passages. Up until now, the virtues of this ideal woman have been mostly outward—in the things she does with her hands—but the Bible now speaks of her spirit and character more directly. She is clothed in a strong spirit of courage, and she exudes the honor she so richly deserves. She is a big soul made bigger by every sacrifice to improve the lot of her family as well as the poor and needy.

> *She is a big soul made bigger by every sacrifice to improve the lot of her family as well as the poor and needy.*

"She shall rejoice in time to come" indicates that if in the present she is preoccupied with her labor and commitments and sometimes fails to rejoice, there is the promise of one day looking back over it all and rejoicing in the fruit of her labor, knowing that if she had it to do all over again, she wouldn't do anything differently. In every life there are some failures, some tragedies, some pain; but how blessed it is to look back over a life well lived and rejoice that you were there living every minute of it and be able to give thanks to God for the strength it produced in your soul. Such is the virtuous woman that is so hard to find. **"She will do him good and not evil all the days of her life."** Proverbs 31:12

Need I lecture you on the virtues of marrying a woman who is clothed in strength of character and honor? If you want a woman who will bring you honor in the gates and will not grow bitter and resentful but will one day look back on the life she spent with you and rejoice in your sojourn together, then it is most imperative that you marry a virtuous woman.

Kindness is not a social tool for her; it is the condition of her heart.

26 She openeth her mouth with wisdom; and in her tongue is the law of kindness.

This woman has been busy in service to her family and others, but she has not failed to develop her own heart and spirit. She is a woman of wisdom. She discerns the good and evil. She knows the ins and outs of the spirit and the human heart. She is not deceived by the world and the devil. Whether she is leaning over her loom or walking in scarlet and silk, she is the same woman of wisdom inside.

And **"in her tongue is the law of kindness."** She is not provoked to be petty and vindictive. She speaks softly where kindness is needed, but she is also **"kind unto the unthankful and to the evil."** Luke6:35 Kindness is not a social tool for her; it is the condition of her heart. She loves her neighbor and her enemies, being bigger than her enemies while making herself lower than her neighbors. Wow! This woman is indeed a soul of great virtue, worth more than a whole barrel of rubies. Later in a man's life this verse takes greater signif-icance. Older women who have demanded their own way from their youth can get really vindictive and controlling. It is in these years that what they have been is made manifest.

Now you know what God values and why it is so hard to find a woman of great virtue.

A young girl will not be gathering wisdom if she is online tweeting and texting and listening to music and idling away her

> *The woman of great virtue gives great and effectual attention to her household.*

time at the mall looking at the latest fashions. Wisdom comes from the fear of the LORD and from the Word of God. You become the kind of music you listen to and the people with whom you hang out. A woman of virtue is not born; she is made from one minute to the next, day after day, and year after year in all of her experiences.

27 She looketh well to the ways of her household, and eateth not the bread of idleness.

This is another biggie. The woman of great virtue gives great and effectual attention to her household, that is, to those who live in her house. That would include children and husband and any old parents living with them. **"Looketh well"** says that her attention is well placed and very effectual toward blessing all under her roof. Looketh to the **"ways"** of her household reveals that her oversight goes deeper than just meeting the physical and emotional needs of the family; she also guides them in their **"ways,"** that is, she leads them in paths of righteousness for his name's sake. She instructs and provides an example that keeps her children walking in the right way, not the wrong way.

She must also instruct her children in a manner that we now call homeschooling. She may find appropriate tutors or arrange for them to be taught by other family members or trusted friends, but she looks well to them in all things.

That will keep her busy, so she **"eateth not the bread of idleness."** What a fantastic, up-to-date way of describing what she is not and what most modern women are! Picture an idle woman. What do idle, bored women do? Why, they eat of course. They munch on this and that all day long. Food becomes a comfort to them, a way of releasing endorphins. So they eat the bread of idleness. It must have been so in Solomon's day as well. A woman with no purpose in life just sat around the house and munched on unleavened bread. Maybe she salted it down or put some honey on it. Or she might have fried it and made barley chips. Wow! Modern-day insight from King Solomon 3,000 years ago.

A busy woman with a purpose doesn't have time to munch, and she is so active that she burns calories like a forest fire burns pine needles.

Once again, you may not mind an idle woman who grows fat in the belly while dawdling away her life on the computer or telephone, but you need to go into marriage with your eyes open. If you want to settle for something less than the best, I am glad that there are guys like you who can love girls like that, because there are more of the idle types than there are of the virtuous types, and they are going to need husbands as well.

Many times I have observed two fat people deeply in love sitting together in twin recliners passing the chips back and forth. Their laughter is contagious and it seems they wouldn't have it any other way. That's average. So be it. But the choice is yours. Know what you are getting into and be happy with the predictable outcome.

A virtuous woman is recognized for her intrinsic worth.

28 Her children arise up, and call her blessed; her husband also, and he praiseth her.

A virtuous woman will never lack praise from her husband or children. She is recognized for her intrinsic worth. It is a sad fact that most mothers, though loved, are not openly praised by their families. Spontaneous praise is generated by a sense of the extraordinary in someone we know and love. We all develop a baseline as to what we expect from people. It is only when someone far exceeds our expectations that we are provoked to spontaneous praise. The virtuous woman generates praise on many accounts.

There is seldom vindication in this life. But the virtuous woman is justified of her children and her grandchildren, and she leaves her mark on generations to come. Reaping can be a wonderful blessing, and it certainly is for the virtuous woman.

29 Many daughters have done virtuously, but thou excellest them all.

This passage is a relief. Solomon acknowledges that **"many,"** not just this one, **"have done virtuously."** I was beginning to get discouraged. At the time when I married my wife she had not yet fully revealed herself to be a match to the virtuous woman described here in Proverbs 31. And as I think about all the young unmarried girls, the only ones I can suppose are as virtuous as the Proverbs 31 woman are the ones I do not know so well. So I am relieved when Solomon acknowledges that the woman he describes excels many who are nonetheless virtuous. We cannot but conclude, and happily so, that the description is an ideal one and it might be impractical for too many of us guys to delay marriage until we have found such a one. That might result in a sharp decrease in population growth and an entire generation of bachelors and old maids.

So, in your search for a help meet, you must keep six things in mind:

1. You should search for a virtuous woman as described in Proverbs 31.

2. If you look closely enough, she will probably come short of full compliance with all the fantastic virtues described here.

3. There is great virtue that does not reach this level of excellence.

4. You have no right to believe that you above all other guys deserve such a woman.

5. Know that you will come to love and desire a woman who is not going to be perfect.

6. Make sure that your love for a woman renders you willing to accept her limitations and allow her space to continue to grow. No one ever buys an apple tree already bearing enough apples to make a pie.

30 Favour is deceitful, and beauty is vain: but a woman that feareth the LORD, she shall be praised.

We now come to Solomon's concluding thoughts regarding our search for a virtuous woman. Thus far, there has been a glaring absence of one key concern for most young men. He has said nothing about her looks. Aren't good looks a matter of great worth? I never dreamed of marrying an ugly woman. Did you? The good queen who wrote this prophecy for her son knew men were of this frame of mind; she knew her son might miss the finest wife if he were not warned that beauty is vain and can hide serious troubles.

"Favour is deceitful." To be favored is to be preferred; the text links favor to beauty. We all favor the beautiful. You know that in school or church with a hundred young girls of marriageable age, a few are favored above the others. If there were a catch-and-keep day where a hundred girls were turned

Love at first sight is lust without wisdom—desire without brains.

loose so a hundred guys could catch the girl of their choice, one or two girls would be chased by twenty-five or more guys. Those girls are favored. The one standing next to the swing set with everybody running past her is not so favored.

The text says, **"favour is deceitful, and beauty is vain,"** linking favour with beauty. I am sixty-seven years old. I have seen many beautiful females in my life and know very well that the devil can come gift-wrapped in a babe's bod, but I still find it unnatural to say beauty is vain. This is a passage you don't have to feel, but you better believe it. The Apostle Peter says that a woman's beauty **"should be the hidden man of the heart, in that which is not corruptible, even the ornament of a meek and quiet spirit, which is in the sight of God of great price."** 1 Peter 3:4 A girl's looks and likability are deceptive because we guys are such suckers for eye candy. **"Lust not after her beauty in thine heart; neither let her take thee with her eyelids."** Proverbs 6:25 When our hormones kick in, the world is transformed into a beautiful place full of hope and promise. Love at first sight has no second sight; it is as blind as a napkin blowing in traffic. Love at first sight is lust without wisdom—desire without brains.

> *I suggest that you get to know many girls— the pretty and the plain—and search for the virtues found here in Proverbs 31.*

Isn't it interesting that all girls—or nearly all—are eventually loved and cherished by some man, no matter how plain they might be, but the plainer girls are never the object of love at first sight. Some guy got to know them and saw something beautiful he wanted to love for the rest of his life. It might have been love after the fifth conversation, or love after observing her playing with the children and taking care of her aging grandparents, or love after reading an article she wrote, or love after spending a week with her on a mission trip, but it is a love that will last through the years of fading beauty.

I have gotten to know a lot of females in my many years of active living, and I have come to a very firm knowledge that some of the greatest treasures come dressed in the plainest packages. I know some lookers that a man would be lucky to avoid and some very plain girls that are as fun as a pool full of kids, and as smart and talented as an entire variety show, filled with interesting conversation and full of fun-loving ways. I know some girls who could walk through Wal-Mart all day long and never have a single guy look at them twice, but once you get to know them you realize they are worth more than a whole truckload of rubies.

On a looks scale of one to ten, only about one out of several hundred is going to be a perfect ten. If we rated the heart and spirit on a scale of one to ten, I would say that among homeschool gals about one out of every ten or twenty is a perfect 10. So what are the odds of those two tens coming together in the same package?

Most guys think beauty is main, but God says it is vain.

Think about it, a woman of great virtue—a woman of qualities that are most praiseworthy and desirable to make a man happy and fulfilled—is more likely to be found in the much larger number of plain girls than in the limited number of extraordinary lookers. Furthermore, while most of the guys are competing for the long eyelashes and rosebud lips, the biggest treasures are unattended, without any suitors, just waiting to become a man's greatest delight. There is no want of virtuous girls; there is just a want of guys wanting them.

I suggest that you get to know many girls—the pretty and the plain—and search for the virtues found here in Proverbs 31. Even though your flesh may be focused on the flesh, if you fix your mind on the mind and soul of the girls, you may be one of the lucky ones who falls in love with an ordinary looking gal with an extraordinary soul and personality, the kind who will love and appreciate you all the way through your aging years and into eternity.

I don't know many men who are disappointed that they will not be married to their wives in heaven. They are anticipating a legitimate separation for a few million years. I can tell you without any pretense at all, if God allowed marriage in heaven and the girls were all number tens, I would choose to enter into eternal covenant with the wife of my youth. We are one in body and soul. It is this knowledge that gives me the liberty to write this book.

The passage says **"beauty is vain."** Most guys think beauty is main, but God says it is vain. Vanity is a great promise rotting into emptiness and bitter futility. It is expectation come up against the coldness of reality. It is a hand that grasped and came back holding nothing. Solomon said vanity is vexation of spirit. Ecclesiastes 1:14 The pursuit of beauty for itself will leave the spirit tired and empty.

I will tell you something you will not be able to relate to, so you can just take my word for it. When a man loves the spirit of a woman, she becomes beautiful to him. Truly, love blinds. It is amazing. I have observed it countless times; a handsome guy married to an almost ugly woman, and he dotes over her like she was a singing, dancing sensation. Think about it—everybody loves their mother, and most mothers are plain and old and fat and wrinkled and yet loved, and the kids can't really tell you if Mother is beautiful or not—she is Mother!

When a man loves the spirit of a woman, she becomes beautiful to him.

The other day my wife pulled out a picture of herself on our honeymoon, and after I gawked at it for a minute, I said, "It is a good thing you don't look like that now or you would wear me down to skin and bone." She smiled with satisfaction and said, "You didn't know what you had, did you?" As I thought about it, the answer I didn't speak was, "No, at the time, I did not realize I was married to a woman of such beauty." Today as I compare the pictures, I realize few people would recognize it was a picture of my sixty-year-old wife forty years earlier. But, truly, today she is, in my mind, much prettier than I thought her to be the day we married. The beauty of youth has been consumed by her forty years of service to me. Each gray hair and each wrinkle came in the midst of many laughs and shared thoughts and experiences. They slipped in unnoticed without ever diminishing her beauty or worth to me. Her spirit I now love far more than I ever enjoyed her body—which was considerable. Now, don't get me wrong, the body thing is not behind us. This old man and old woman can still rattle the foundations and make the kids stop knocking on the back door and scurry home pretending not to have heard Mom and Pop celebrating again.

"**Beauty is vain: but a woman that feareth the LORD, she shall be praised.**" A woman that fears the LORD shall be praised. I guess I just did that. "**Her children arise up, and call her blessed; her husband also, and he praiseth her.**" Proverbs 31:28 A woman who loves and honors God will love her husband even when he is not lovely. That kind of gal will sustain a marriage through the barren times and bring it to a merry mountaintop at last.

31 Give her of the fruit of her hands; and let her own works praise her in the gates.

The final verse in this virtuous woman description looks back over "**the fruit of her hands**" and commands that a man should allow his wife to benefit from her own labor. Solomon anticipates that some men might think to hide away a hard-working and productive woman, benefiting from her labor but not allowing her to take credit for her work. It is proper for a woman to enjoy praise in the gates.

It is proper for a woman to enjoy praise in the gates.

Wow! This is good! Sorry, I get carried away with the beauty and psychological depth of the text.

Many men are so insecure they will not allow their wives to succeed in their own right. If a woman makes it or earns it, she should be trusted with the praise and fruit of her labor.

Excuse me again. This is so contrary to the way I was brought up and to so many books.

A Christian wife is commanded by God to submit to her husband, but it never commands a husband to submit his wife to himself. A woman's voluntary submission to her husband is an act of obedience to God and honor toward her husband, and a commitment to a form of family government that makes a home run smoothly. It is not a statement of her inferiority or inability.

Weak men are afraid of strong women and favor a doctrine that keeps all women away from the wheels of power. The answer is not to chain the women but for men to outperform them. However, it is best when there is no competition, rather, the man and woman are a team and share in the responsibility and the rewards of their common labor. After all, that is what a help meet is—a woman suited to help the man fulfill his goals and visions.

Understanding these things will help you make a wiser decision in choosing a help meet.

A woman who loves and honors God will love her husband even when he is not lovely.

For this God is our God for ever and ever: he will be our guide even unto death.

Psalm 48:14

Bible Studies
for
New Couples

by Ben Sargent

Use this guide to learn together some basic principles that will help you and your prospective bride build a glorious, God-honoring marriage.

LESSON 1

I. It is common today for Christians to be encouraged to seek counseling, talk to their pastor, their mentor etc., but is that God's position? Where should a child of God go for instruction, encouragement, for counsel? Where is the bedrock truth that is not influenced by time, culture or man's sin?

What is the final authority for a Christian?

1. Is the Bible the Word of God? Psalms 12:6-7, 119:89; Matthew 24:35; 1 Peter 1:25, 26

2. Can it be trusted literally?
   Job 13:15, 23:12; Psalms 33:4, 118:8, 119:160

3. What effect does the Word have in a Christian's life?
   John 17:17; Acts 20:32; Colossians 3:16;
   1 Thessalonians 2:13

4. Who has the responsibility to know the Word?
   Psalms 119:9-11; 2 Timothy 2:15; 1 John 2:14

5. How do I learn it? Isaiah 28:9-10; 1 Corinthians 14:34-35;
   1 Timothy 4:13; 2 Timothy 2:15

For a couple to be successful they need to have a source of truth that is relevant in every area of their lives. Without an anchor the ship called the USS Marriage drifts aimlessly with every current or strong wind until it finally is beaten upon the rocks and utterly destroyed.

LESSON 2

II. As with everything God creates, he does so with decency and order (1 Corinthians 14:40). The home is no different.

What is God's structure for the home?

1. What is the husband's role? Matthew 1:19;
   Ephesians 5:23, 25, 28, 33; Colossians 3:19;
   1 Corinthians 7:3-4, 11:3; 1 Peter 3:7

      a. How should a husband care for the physical
         well-being of his wife? Ephesians 5:28-29; 1 Peter 3:7

      b. How does a man handle his wife who will not obey?
         Ephesians 5:25-27; 1 Peter 3:8-9

Husbands are commanded to love their wives, not to make them obey or submit. The command from God to husbands is that they love their wives. God's commandments to the wives about their husbands are between the wives and God.

2. What is a wife's role? Proverbs 31:10-31; Ephesians 5:33;
   Colossians 3:18; 1 Timothy 5:14; Titus 2:4-5; 1 Peter 3:1-6

      a. Who would obey a man – what if he's wrong?
         Titus 2:5; 1 Peter 3:6

      b. Is a woman commanded to submit to a man?
         Ephesians 5:22; Colossians 3:18; 1 Timothy 2:11;
         1 Peter 3:1, 5

236

Becoming the woman God intends her to be and the woman her husband needs her to be will cause him to love her. A wife's conversation (speech, attitude, and body language) is critical to the spirit in the home. God's commandments to husbands are between the husbands and God.

3. How should Christians raise their children?
   Deuteronomy 6:7, 11:19, 31:19; Psalms 127:3;
   Proverbs 1:8, 4:1, 13:1, 15:5, 22:6; Ephesians 6:4;
   Titus 1:6, 2:4

   a. What is a child? Exodus 30:14; Leviticus 27:3, 5;
      Numbers 1:3, 18, 20, 14:29

   b. Should grown children obey their parents in the Lord?
      Ephesians 6:1-4; Titus 2:4

From the inception of the Law, offspring were counted as adults in the Old Testament for accountability and census taking in preparation for war at twenty. They were no longer referred to as children. They are independent decision-makers, held accountable to God and society (Old Testament Law), not parents.

God's provision of roles in a family was not to minimize the importance of any member, but rather, to provide a framework for family success. This design was for the triumph of the family over evil and for the glory of God.

LESSON 3

III. Some young women see bitterness in their parents' relationship and it makes them gun-shy about marriage and distrustful of men generally. Bitterness is to be avoided without exception, so it would be wise to observe a potential mate's conversation toward others, particularly her dad.

Can anyone who carries bitterness in their heart make a fit spouse?

1. What are the associations of bitterness?
   Numbers 5; Deuteronomy 32:21-25; Jeremiah 2:19; Acts 8:23; Romans 3:10-18

2. How can bitterness impact the home?
   Psalms 64:3; Proverbs 14:10; Jeremiah 4:18; Colossians 3:19; James 3:10-15;

3. When is bitterness justified?
   Ephesians 4:31; Hebrews 12:14-16

The Christian landscape is littered with marriages that were destroyed due to a single root of bitterness that sprang up like a Kudzu vine and choked the life from a previously successful couple. It is better not to purchase the field that is already overrun with Kudzu when you're trying to grow grapes.

LESSON 4

IV. It is often stated that couples struggle over two primary things: communication and money. It is unlikely that any two people have the exact same approach about money even if they are raised in the same house. Consequently, it would be prudent to converse regularly about the approach of the home finances.

Does the Bible really teach about finance?

1. What are some biblical admonitions about money?
   Matthew 6:24; Luke 16:11; 1 Timothy 6:10

2. What is the purpose of money?
   Genesis 23:9-16; Deuteronomy 2:6; Ecclesiastes 7:12

3. How can I honor the Lord with money?
   Mark 12:41-44; Luke 12:48; 2 Corinthians 8:1-5;
   Ephesians 4:28

Money is a tool for purchasing power, the ability to be a blessing to others, to provide for the ministry, and to glorify God. Loving it causes destruction; sowing it well reaps a wonderful harvest.

Lesson 5

V. Samson and Solomon failed to become what God intended them to be. Both married women they were expressly forbidden to marry. Christians are not to be unequally yoked with unbelievers, so it is prudent to ensure any potential bride's relationship with the Master.

How can I determine if someone knows the Lord as their Savior?

1. Does the Bible teach that we can see another's relationship with God? Matthew 7:16-20, 12:33; Mark 4:3-20; Romans 6:22, 7:4-6; Galatians 5:22; Ephesians 5:9-13

    a. Can/should a person be sure they are saved? Ephesians 1:13, 4:30; 1 John 2:24-25, 5:3

2. Is there a difference between knowing Jesus lived and knowing him? John 17:3; Acts 1:15-20, 9:1-21, 26:1-28

3. What does it mean to be lost? Psalms 58:3; Isaiah 53:6, 59:2; Romans 3:10-20, 6:23; Galatians 3:10; James 2:10

4. What does it mean to be saved/born again? John 3:1-18, 10:9, 14:6; Acts 2:21, 4:12, 16:30-31; Romans 5:9-10; 2 Corinthians 5:21; Ephesians 2:8-9

Does this woman to whom you are attracted really know the Lord herself? Is she saved or just really nice, really attractive, and really lost? Loving someone to whom you are attracted does not mean you should marry them.

LESSON 6

VI. The disciples of Christ never asked if they were to be involved in the ministry to bring glory to their Lord. They got to work teaching, table wiping, and tent making. They looked for ways to honor the one who had bled to death in their place.

Should every Christian be actively involved in the ministry, or is that just for those who hear a specific call?

1. Who should be involved in personal soul winning and presenting the gospel? Matthew 28:19; Mark 16:15; Romans 10:15; 1 Corinthians 1:17, 9:16

2. What are the gifts in the scriptures? Romans 12:4-8; 1 Corinthians 12:4-11; Ephesians 4:7-16

3. What does the Bible teach about church offices in the New Testament? Romans 12:4-5; 1 Timothy 3:1-13

4. Were we merely saved from hell, or is there a bigger purpose? Psalms 23:3, 106:8; Isaiah 66:5; Acts 26:16; Romans 9:23-24; Ephesians 1:3-6, 12, 14; 1 Thessalonians 2:11-12; 1 Peter 5:6-10; 1 John 2:12; Jude 1:24-25

Jesus implored his disciples to keep his commandments (John 14:15, 15:10). He commanded us to go. He provides gifts (Romans 12:6-8), administrations and operations (1 Corinthians 12:5-6), opportunities (Acts chapters 2, 10, & 16), and the leadership of the Holy Ghost (Romans 8:14). Irrespective of our background, blue-collar (Peter the fisherman, Paul the tentmaker), or white (Matthew the tax collector), a Christian family should be about their father's business (Luke 2:49).

LESSON 7

VII. Years ago the United States military members were admired for their self-discipline. This discipline came from continual preparation and carefulness in their personal conduct. Christian men are tender warriors who seek self-discipline for the glory of God.

Why is it important for Christian men to practice self-discipline?

1. What does a Christian man look like from the outside? Psalm 1; 1 Corinthians 9:24-27; Ephesians 5:15-17; Galatians 5:22-26; 2 Timothy 2:3-5; Titus 1:8, 2:2

2. What type of things should a young man discipline himself to be cautious about? Proverbs 2:16, 5:3, 5:20, 6:24, 7:5, 20:1, 16, 23:27, 27:13; Isaiah 5:11, 22, 28:7; Galatians 5:1; Ephesians 5:18-21; 2 Peter 2:20-21

3. Should all Christian men study the Bible? Psalms 119:9-11, 89, 101, 105, 130, 133, 140, 148, 160-162, 138:2; 2 Timothy 2:15

A combat warrior stealthily moving through the jungle watches where his feet go to avoid stepping on an IED; he exercises and hardens his body for warfare and constantly trains and prepares for the next mission by study and practice. Christian men are in a warfare (2 Corinthians 10:4; 1 Timothy 1:18) with a real adversary (1 Peter 5:8). Self-discipline keeps a man of God focused and busy.

Finally, my brethren, be strong in the Lord, and in the power of his might.

Put on the whole armour of God, that ye may be able to stand against the wiles of the devil.

For we wrestle not against flesh and blood,

but against principalities, against powers,

against the rulers of the darkness of this world,

against spiritual wickedness in high places.

Wherefore take unto you the whole armour of God, that ye may be able to withstand in the evil day, and having done all, to stand.

Stand therefore, having your loins girt about with truth, and having on the breastplate of righteousness;

And your feet shod with the preparation of the gospel of peace;

Above all, taking the shield of faith, wherewith ye shall be able to quench all the fiery darts of the wicked.

And take the helmet of salvation, and the sword of the Spirit, which is the word of God.

Praying always with all prayer and supplication in the Spirit, and watching thereunto with all perseverance and supplication for all saints;

Ephesians 5:10-18

Created to Need a Help Meet

Mike's new book can help men understand how to be the husband that God created them to be. Man up!!! ***Book.***

> Available in: single volumes, case quantities, and on audio.

Created to Be His Help Meet

What God is doing through this book is amazing. Has it provoked you to want to be the help meet God created you to be? We pray so. If it has blessed you (and your beloved) then consider passing the blessing on to someone you love by purchasing *Created To Be His Help Meet* for them. ***Book.***

> Available in: single volumes, case quantities, and on audio.

Preparing to Be a Help Meet

Being a good help meet starts long before marriage. It is a mindset, a learned habit, a way of life established as a young unmarried girl—or at least that's the way it should be. For unmarried and married women. ***Book.***

> Available in: single volumes, case quantities, and on audio.

Holy Sex

Michael Pearl takes his readers through a refreshing journey of Biblical texts, centered in the Song of Solomon. This sanctifying look at the most powerful passion God ever created will free the reader from false guilt and inhibition. ***Book.***

Only Men

Michael Pearl speaks directly and frankly to men about their responsibilities as husbands. Wives should not listen to this message. We don't want you taking advantage of your man. ***1 CD.***

Pornography: Road to Hell

Michael addresses the deadly scourge of pornography head-on. He shows how repentance toward God and the power of the gospel of Jesus Christ can break the bondage of this wicked perversion. ***12 page booklet.***

Good and Evil

Award winning graphic novel, 330 pages of dazzling full color art work telling the Bible story chronologically from Genesis to Revelation. Written by Michael Pearl and drawn by Danny Bulanadi, a retired Marvel Comic Book artist. Now in over 30 languages, popular with missionaries and youth workers, this book has tremendous appeal to all ages and cultures–great as Sunday School curriculum. ***Book.***

Available in: single volumes, case quantities, and multiple languages.

Knife & Tomahawk Throwing for Fun

Michael Pearl demonstrates and teaches knife and tomahawk throwing. ***1 DVD.***

Becoming a Man

This message is for parents concerned about raising their boys up to be men, and it is for fathers who never learned to be real men. *1 CD.*

Becoming Tempered Steel

Joshua Steele talks to young men about being a man and a minister of the Gospel. Highly recommended by Michael Pearl. *1 DVD.*